Adolescence: The Confusing Years

Revised

ADOLESCENCE:
the confusing years!

G. Lorin Swanson

TECHNOMIC
PUBLISHING CO., INC.

LANCASTER · BASEL

Published in the Western Hemisphere by
Technomic Publishing Company, Inc.
851 New Holland Avenue
Box 3535
Lancaster, Pennsylvania 17604 U.S.A.

Distributed in the Rest of the World by
Technomic Publishing AG

Printed in the United States of America
10 9 8 7 6 5 4 3 2 1

Main entry under title:
  Adolescence: The Confusing Years—Revised Edition

A Technomic Publishing Company book
Bibliography: p.
Includes index p. 197

Library of Congress Card No. 87-71932
ISBN No. 87762-550-6

TO MY JESSICA LEE

(God's gift and my delight)

To our children,
Look to this day
For yesterday is but a dream,
And tomorrow is only a vision.

But today well lived
Makes every yesterday
A dream of happiness,
And every tomorrow
A vision of hope.

from the Sanskrit

TABLE OF CONTENTS

CHAPTER SIX

THE WELL-KEPT SECRET   **121**

CHAPTER SEVEN

SEX IS ONLY A THREE LETTER WORD   **141**

PREFACE

My six-year old and I were in the kitchen. Jessica was balancing on the work-island, and I was ready to say, "You're going to fall." I don't know why, but instead I put my arms around her. We embraced each other.

"Don't ever go away from me," I said as I held her.

"What do you mean?" she asked. "Do you mean go away while I'm in school?"

"No," I replied. My thoughts of her going away were of teenage suicide. Running away. Escaping life by using drugs. Getting pregnant. Being afraid of me.

"I mean when you grow up."

"Ohhh . . ." she said deep in thought. "But I have to. I HAVE to go away." She hesitated. "But I'll live with you for a while."

My heart sank. "I know. Just promise me that you'll visit."

Her arms grew tighter around me. "But you've already had me for all of these years."

I told her, "Thank you."

Love may have once meant "Never having to say you're sorry," but it doesn't anymore. Five hundred thousand adolescents will try to kill themselves each year. Five thousand will succeed. They will kill themselves at the rate of one every 90 minutes. Up to 1.2 million kids will run away, and 600,000 will become prostitutes. One out of four teenagers will drop out of high school. Ten million have dropped out since 1975. Twelve million girls will engage in sex every year. Six hundred and eighty thousand will have babies. One half of all welfare cases will involve children with children. Within two years, 30 percent will be pregnant again. At least once a month, 2,700,000 kids will light up a joint, 390,000 will use cocaine, and 66 percent of all adolescents will take more than one drink.

It's going to be a busy year.

I first wrote this book five years ago because I believed there was a need. I was afraid if I got too far away from those years I would not remember. I was 27 at the time. I am older now, and I wanted to dismiss those years. I wanted to forget they had ever happened. This is how hard the adolescent years are.

Five years later the need is even greater. The topics discussed at that time are still with us, and they are multiplying. This is a book for the parent and for the adolescent. It is for anyone who would like to listen. I am writing as a parent, but I am also using experiences and poetry I wrote during my adolescent years.

We all have our own opinions, just as I have mine. My opinions will surface throughout the book, and you have the right to judge them. That's to be expected. I am not an expert in any given field, but then . . . who is? If I were an expert I would have the answer to life. That answer is not mine to give. It is yours. The purpose of the book is to open communication and give information. The frosting on the cake is if the parent and child can sit down together and discuss it, interjecting their own thoughts and feelings.

Adolescents are very complex human beings. They are a kid trying to become an adult practically overnight. It is not easy, and it never will be. I would like for us to understand the adolescent and young adult differently from how they are portrayed in many books. I want us to feel the frustration, the confusion, and love as teenagers feel it. But I also want us to look objectively at what is occurring at this time. We may think statistics are only numbers, but they are not. These statistics are now our children.

The only way they will be able to escape from becoming one of these statistics is if we help them. They cannot do it alone. Reach into your heart and put out your hand. Give them the strength they need to overcome all that lies before them.

Our children are only with us for a short time. Thank them for sharing their lives with us.

ACKNOWLEDGEMENTS

There are a few people I would like to thank for making this book possible. My first thanks goes to Technomic Publishing Co. and all who worked on this project with me. They helped fulfill a goal of a lifetime. I believe I speak for all of us in saying we hope the book will be beneficial for all parties concerned, in helping to bring about a new understanding of adolescents and the hardships they must face. Thanks to Melvyn A. Kohudic, publisher; Joseph Eckenrode, editor; Jerry Melson, editor first edition; Anthony Deraco, production manager; and Richard Dunn, vice-president of marketing.

I would also like to thank my husband Daryl for the hours of proofreading he put in and for never saying, "Do I have to read it AGAIN?" Thanks to my daughter Jessica who sensed the importance of my writing the book and who didn't complain too much when I typed instead of playing "Barbies." Thanks to my friend Cory who saw me through those years and stuck with me as a friend. (Yes, we DID make it out of adolscence and survived!) Janie, Barb, Kathy, Denise and Debbie: I treasure you all. Thanks to my parents.

Last, but probably most important . . . I thank the many sources I interviewed but who wished anonymity in order to remain totally truthful. You know who you are, and I am grateful. It is through honesty such as yours that a better understanding can be gained.

ABOUT THE AUTHOR

G. Lorin Swanson is a successful writer and businesswoman. She has written for radio, television and newspapers. Her credits include a number of feature stories for the *Minneapolis Star and Tribune,* a national column on patient care for the *Journal of Nursing Care,* and comedy material for a television pilot. She is the author of *Silent Rage,* an unpublished expose of a U.S. chemical company's efforts to market a rat poison through the South Korean government. In addition, Ms. Swanson has created advertising literature for C.O.M.B. Co. of Minnesota, as well as for two smaller companies of which she is part owner.

Ms. Swanson received her education at the University of Minnesota and the University of Oklahoma, and has also studied communications and broadcasting at the Brown Institute, Minneapolis.

She has held a number of positions at the University of Minnesota Hospitals, including Pharmacy Technician, Ward Secretary for the Child Psychology Unit, and Clinic Coordinator and Office Specialist of the Emergency Room.

G. Lorin Swanson is married and the mother of five children.

CHAPTER ONE

A Time For Feeling

*A*DOLESCENCE. TRULY, A very important time in our lives. It is a confusing time. It is a time for growing, a time for learning, and a time to discover the essence of who we are.

I have come to the conclusion there really is no way of getting around hard and trying times, for they come into our lives for a reason. They come to teach us all about ourselves.

What causes the process to be so difficult is that every single, minute aspect of adolescence is bombarded at us. There is no time to grasp it, to head it off or to even engulf it as a new feeling or experience.

Adolescence is the period of time between childhood and adulthood, the drifting in between. Our feelings are explosive. We want only two things: we want still to be a child and to be cared for, and we want to be an adult with total independence. No matter how hard we strive to hold on, we are caught in the middle.

We realize this cannot be avoided, so what is the answer? Perhaps the best answer is to simply try our hardest to understand what is really taking place. Which in itself, is not an easy task. As for myself, I don't know how on earth I managed to muddle through adolescence without killing myself. Hopefully, we all have that inborn sense telling us to back off when the fire gets too hot. And we get through, somehow. And we have learned, and we have shared, and we have come to know and be ourselves.

> *Staring into your eyes.*
> *you bring me into your world.*
> *I am a part of your thoughts*
> *floating among the clouds.*
>
> *Let me be an autumn leaf*
> *swirling to my fancy.*
> *Turning the colors*
> *to the throb of the sun.*

1

I am an eagle
  soaring to my destiny
  which you are a part of.
You make me want to belong
  to stay for awhile.

But with the seasons
  I will also change.
And you must understand
  who I am.

Please turn the colors with me.
And we will change into one.

              (16 years old)

SUDDEN AWARENESS OF EMOTIONS

One of the most dramatic things happening to us during adolescence is that we become aware of our feelings and emotions. It's like nothing else we have ever experienced. We feel! We feel about everything! These sensations pour through us like a wild fire fed with gasoline. We have trouble understanding these feelings, and sometimes, we don't even know what to do with them.

We feel happy. We feel sad. We now know how to love in such an exciting new way. We are confused, angry, and lonely. We are capable of feeling every single feeling we as human beings can feel. And these feelings . . . they come on to us with a new, unfamiliar intensity.

The drops of dew
  awakened my senses.
My arms reached out
  and caressed the sun.

The sun rose to its satisfaction
  and with it rose my mind.

Made me aware
  of its beauty
Kept me high.

The sun slowly but strong,
  turned the earth on
  made it mellow   warm.
It drowned out the fighting
  and what was cold.

We live by the sun.
We live on it.

(17 years old).

I discovered poems I had written during my adolescent years—written and hidden away. I will use these to help us understand what we are trying to discover and learn about adolescence.

I was shocked when I read through them. I was just a kid. Kids don't count, do they? I felt so strong about so many things! Sometimes we forget this intensity as we grow older. And it's such an interesting, lovely intensity—one I wish we could hold onto a while longer.

Her tears often come in patterns
Patterns,
  life plays with.
Time;
  moves along slowly
  with its rhythm and movement.

Fog lifts from the sun.
Where do I belong?
Where does anyone?

A tree stands at attention
  securely placed
And forgotten in seclusion.
A night star falls
and paints it silver.

Dark footsteps in the sand
leading out to a midnight sea.
Where do they belong?

A face peers through a window
  stained with tears.
A silent cry
  in the stillness of the night
A broken heart
  smothered in loneliness . . .
Where does it belong?

(16 years old)

Objects, feelings and persons we have taken for granted suddenly come alive with a powerful thrust. We are now capable of viewing everything through a different perspective. We can now begin to understand and recognize true beauty, sadness and loneliness for the first time. And it hurts.

A single tree standing in seclusion awakens our inner feelings, and we imagine all the crooked torment or passionate love it took to make and carefully design that tree. All the rain, the windstorms, the piercing sun . . . we are even capable of feeling for a single tree.

We reach out to others and try to tell them how fantastic it all is. But they do not understand. "A tree? What about a tree? Did it fall down or something . . . what did it hit?"

"No, it's the shape. Don't you see how cool it is? There isn't one alike! They're all different! See how that one branch reaches out to . ."

"Hmmm. That's nice. Did you finish your homework?"

"No . . . not yet. I just thought . . ."

"You're not going to the soccer game unless you finish your homework."

Maybe they did see this tree a long time ago. Maybe they did appreciate its beauty. Perhaps they lost the sporadic impulse to love it just as it is. So what do we feel? We feel confused and probably a little lonely, realizing for the first time we are the only ones drinking in a marvelous, wonderful feeling.

SENSE OF BELONGING

We as human beings have a deep-rooted need to belong. We need to fit in somewhere. Anywhere. And sometimes, our homes and our families do not provide us with this. If such is the case, we will look elsewhere.

Routines can be boring to some, but they are essential for children. They need to know there are things in life they can count on. Everybody is busy. Our chores never end. But we need to sit down and chat.

We once took care of an eleven-year-old child. We were just a pit-stop in her life, but I know she'll never forget. She had been bounced around her entire life. What we gave her wasn't complicated. It was part of our routine, our consistency—the busy kitchen. Mom trying to get dinner on the table, shouting, "Can you set the table? I forgot the vegetable again. Can you believe it?" Everybody laughs. "Okay . . . are we ready? Call everybody!" We sit down to dinner.

We asked her about her day and what she had learned. She grinned from ear to ear. She couldn't stop talking. She was thrilled. Thrilled, she was a part of something. She belonged at our table. But what was astounding to her was that she mattered.

She couldn't believe we took baths at a certain time during the evening, we read and helped her with her homework. We tucked her in at night, gave her a hug, and didn't tell her she was a baby if she wanted to sleep with a stuffed animal. If a child wants to sleep with a stuffed animal . . . there is a need to sleep with a stuffed animal.

We take these things for granted. We all need to belong. We need it in order to deal with our confusing, hectic lives. Sometimes we think life is so simple for them at this age. It isn't, it is very complicated and confusing. If we as parents cannot recognize this need and provide our children with it, then it is we who must learn.

> *No one seems*
> *to have the time anymore.*
> *Always in a rush*
> *never stopping to see*
> *That there are some really,*
> *beautiful things.*
>
> *Like people.*
> *You have to see them.*
> *Know them.*
> *Figure them out.*
>
> *So many people don't take the time*
> *to even know themselves.*
> *I feel for them*
> *I feel for you.*
> *Are you happy or sad?*
> *Does it make a difference to you?*
>
> *Turn around,*
> *see what's behind you.*
> *Take a look at what is beside you.*
> *Most of all,*
> *take a look at you.*
> *Take the time.*
>
> *(16 years old)*

FRUSTRATION

We are also aware of time moving by very slowly at this age. As we grow older it travels more quickly, but for now . . . every day seems like an eternity.

Through our new awareness of time we recognize there truly is an end in sight. We realize life does not go on forever and ever. It brings on a new anxiety. We feel we had better get moving somewhere, anywhere, and we do not understand it. We feel the urgency, we want to accomplish, but how do we do this when we feel confined? We need our freedom, but our freedom does not come to us until we are a few years down the road. So what do we feel? We feel very FRUSTRATED.

Our tears are no longer those shed from a bump or a bruise. They are real. They are very real, and they come like a torrent of rain flooding the very depths of our being. And we are again, confused. Because sometimes these are tears only we can understand, and at other times, we don't even know their meaning.

We want to shout, "Hey out there! Doesn't ANYBODY understand what is going on here? What is happening to me?" And from this we receive our very first glimpse of what standing on our own two feet really means.

INDIVIDUALITY

People come . . . they go.
According to the wind.
Some come like a wildfire
*   spreading their wings*
Others; like a soft summer day.

But you . . .
Came with wings
*   filtering through my heart*
Gently covering me with your cloak
*   of sometimes sadness.*

To the extremes you are!
A hot breath of love
Or maybe a winter's day.

I have watched . . . listened
through the seasons of your madness
And have yet . . . to only see
my smile reaching yours.

(16 years old)

Traveling through adolescence we are mesmerized by the individuality of the human nature. We no longer envision others as either young or old, fat or thin. We now have the ability to judge people according to our own values.

We are allowed our own true reactions. We are not compelled to like everybody and everything because it is good for us. Everybody doesn't have to like us. (This is something we will discuss in chapter two.)

While we were children we responded to our parents inward and outward reactions. We liked what they liked and disliked accordingly. However, during adolescence we are able to reason with ourselves, and we are able to act out a suitable response. But there will be times when we may go a little overboard, and this is when our loved ones raise their hands in disbelief. "I just don't understand you!" How many times have we heard that one? Chances are, it's true. We don't even understand ourselves.

DISCOVERY

We are drawn like a magnet to discovery. We are entranced with entire concepts, and sometimes we get going so fast it can be difficult to stop and even think. We may find ourselves peering under a rock we played on just a few years ago. But this time, we see the rock as something totally new and different. We think it is so wonderful! We want to understand this colorful rock. We now see the mud as textured, wondering how it got that way.

Even the beetle bug becomes intricate, and we sit and poke at it to see if we can get it to move. We want to know WHY. We want to know WHY, so we can better understand ourselves. We want to discover. We need to discover everything within our outstretched reach.

Sweet smell of earth's new day
accompany me on my journey.
Far away . . . near I will be
next to you, my love.

Share with me the glow in your eyes
on this brand new day!
Holding hands, laughing in the wind,
you and I
Partners to each other.

Green buds growing with the season
seeing life so new and fresh!
And I, seeing you for the first time,
show me the newness of love.

Hand in hand we shall journey on
to find new days to come.
Conscious to each other's thoughts,
we shall find what we are looking for
to bind us into one.

(16 years old)

FEELINGS OF LOVE

In a sense, that fresh breath of love we ever so lightly grasped in our fingertips during adolescence becomes habit forming. This feeling is one of the most important feelings we will ever have in our lives. And unfortunately, during adolescence is the only time in our lives we will not have to search for it. It will find us whether we want it to or not. It can come to us suddenly and then disappear . . . and we're on to the next discovery of a human being.

One day I had no interest whatsoever. The next day I was chasing them all over camp. I was showing off for him. He would smile (it was a goofy smile), and try to show off for me. My girlfriend and I made up all sorts of games to catch their attention. We had to test their interest.

There were two of us girls and two boys. It didn't matter they were the only two boys at the vacation camp. When the opportunity arises, you have to go for it. We told them to meet us at a specific time at a certain place. We made them pay us a quarter first before we told them.

And then, just because they were such good sports about it and actually came up with a quarter, we told them we might even kiss them.

My girlfriend chickened out. I offered her fifty cents. Still no go. I never did find out how long they waited for us in the rain, in the dark, in the cold. We beat them at volleyball the next day, and our interest waned.

As an adult, I am envious. The adolescent's feeling of love is so explosive, so exciting! It's too bad our scientists have not found a way to bottle this feeling for us . . . what a lift it would give us during our middle years! But, alas, we are only given this opportunity once, during our adolescent years. So savour it, adolescents. Savour this very special moment in time.

> . . . *small smiles*
> *Somehow knowing all the while*
> *Paradise has to come to an end.*
> *Regretfully,*
>   *time*
>   *you can never bend.*
>
> *You put it in a package,*
> *You mail it to a friend,*
> *But love and kisses*
> *You can never, never send.*
>
>   *(21 years old)*

While I went through adolescence, I can't count the times I felt the feeling of love. It was like being on a roller coaster or being manic depressive, one or the other. Up one minute . . . down the next. Was it a crush? No, it was love. I could fall in love at the drop of a hat. Just like all of us during this time.

> *You brushed past me*
> *like a warm*
> *gentle breeze.*
>
> *Just going on . . .*
> *In your quiet way.*
>
> *Maybe I caught your eye.*
> *Could there be a chance?*
> *You were as lonely as I?*
>
> *It seemed so natural*
> *so uncomplicated*
> *So simple*
> *that I should love you.*
>
> *(16 years old)*

Being such a smart adult I could say, "That wasn't LOVE . . . it was probably infatuation. Yes, that's what it was." But I would be wrong. I was in love all right. But now that I have traveled through the aging process, my concept of what love is has drastically changed. It's grown with a confusing complexity. I must now analyze it in order for it to be real.

> *It's funny.*
> *But I think I found you.*
>
> *Little did I know*
> *you would be sitting on a park bench*
> *waiting for love to stroll your way.*
>
> *By a lake*
> *so calm and quiet*
> *Just meeting and knowing*
> *eternity is forever.*
> *It shall always be for real*
> *What I shall live for.*
>
> *Your touch*
> *a soft hand*
> *a loving heart*
> *I was so spellbound by your reality.*

All I could mumble . . .
Hello love.

(16 years old)

So I must look back and respect this feeling of love I had so long ago,
and not be envious of it . . . but be glad I even had it.

SPIRIT

Today's a brand new day!
Couldn't feel finer
Than I already am.

The sun was shining brightly
Through the downpour of rain.

(18 years old)

Well, I must have been feeling pretty happy that day. During our
adolescent years we are blessed with such an exciting spirit.
Sometimes, or probably most of the time, our parents feel like they're
trying to train a wild horse. Notice I didn't say "break?" Of all the
things that connect us as human beings, our inner spirit is what can
make or break us. This is, in fact, probably the most important
aspect of adolescence. This is where we can go either right or wrong.

It is a hearty, robust thing, this spirit inside of us. It can take a lot
of push and shove (God knows how we try to test it). But we must
realize it does have limitations. We can break this spirit if we go
after it day after day – trying to take away, chisel away, until there is
nothing left. If we take this spirit away from our children . . . we are
abusing them. This is a form of abuse we have not recognized. We, as
parents, must realize it is we who must limit ourselves.

Usually we think of this spirit as rebellion, resilience, being
negative or destructive. It's only stretching. It has to try its wings. It
too, needs to get up and walk around the room. We don't confine
infants because we are afraid they will hurt themselves, we confine
infants because it is convenient for us.

It is convenient for us if our children do everything we say. It is convenient for us if they act like we think they should. Do you know
what can happen when things are too convenient for us?

Things are never what they appear to be. When children do everything we say, we don't know what they are thinking. They can agree
with us, make things nice . . . but do we really know where they are?
They can be with people we don't want them to be with. They can lie,

and we will never know they have lied. They are not dumb, they are very smart. They can cover their tracks like you can't believe. They can make it appear they were someplace when they really weren't. We can think they are tired when actually they're stoned.

These years can be very trying. I realize only too well how trying these years can be. Let's just say that in my situation, I know for a fact my daughter is going to be more daring, more stubborn and more spirited than I ever was. At the age of two she lay in her crib and screamed, "Meanie Mommie!" I don't even know where she learned the word "mean."

So what is this spirit, this life inside? It is our own special light, a light we must keep burning at all costs. And just how important is this spirit? Picture a pound and a half baby. My Jessica was born three and a half months early. She was given a 5 percent chance to live.

As she lay in the isolette, day after day, month after month, I stood beside her and watched. All I could do is watch. In the beginning, she almost shriveled away. Her shin was hanging off her tiny, bird-like bones, and I watched in agony as the nurses tried to find her veins to draw blood. My baby screamed, and I knew she was in pain. Would she, could she, even stay alive? The spirit inside ME said yes, but she went on struggling to live, fighting off infections, weight loss and death.

But there was an inner light, something inside of her that continued on and grew stronger. It said, it shouted, I WANT TO LIVE. I will give her the credit, it was her spirit, not me or the doctors and nurses who brought her through 76 days of intensive care. Medicine can only do so much, it does not give us the will to live.

We shouldn't have to go through such an extreme in order to see this light. It is in each one of us, but it shines brightest in our children. We must allow them the freedom to be themselves, no matter how hard and trying the times may get. Usually this means sacrifice on our part, but really, going into parenthood we must expect this. We must deal with it on a human level. We need that sense of adventure, something new and exciting to draw us into each and every new day. Adventure makes life IMPORTANT to us . . . it increases our knowledge. If we increase our knowledge, we bring with it new ideas. This is what adds to the human race.

There will be times when we will not realize what is at stake. We are not playing with toys or our favorite animal; we are affecting and nurturing another human life. How we react to this life and actively participate during these years will have an affect on our children the remainder of their lives.

I thank you for all the memories you have left me.
My childhood, so happy and old fashioned . . .
But letting me grow up
When I was ready to accept the challenge.

The city
So old and dirty.
But yet, I am a part of its dust!
Always coming back for more pieces of my life
Picking away at the puzzle
And finding there's always a piece to be found here
In my city.

All the memories
the present and future
are to be found.
And I know their hiding place!

(17 years old)

You see, this spirit, this beautiful thing, turns into something. If this spirit is nurtured properly along the way, there will come a time when we can DRAW from it. It will develop into an important asset called STRENGTH. And this spirit . . . it even goes beyond strength. That little light that shines within actually becomes our very own self-esteem.

FEAR

Here I lie . . . completely motionless
My back flush to the stiff, straight wall
Blindly staring into a darkened space
Which can only speak of long eternity.

My image . . . blurred
And caught within the borders of a mirror
Sorrowfully reflects my empty life
And projects it as a fantasy.

Colored lights flash on marbled floor
Brightly lighting me . . .
As the only actor in my life.
I take the lead of being
The dulled image of myself.

Nature being the only truth
And a withered flower as my only friend.

Colored lights dim.
The marbled floor vanishes.
The mirror blackens,
And I am left with reality's cold loneliness.

(16 years old)

Now enters a very helpless and frightening feeling. We are afraid. We are afraid of so many things, but I think what terrifies us the most is the uncertainty of all that lies ahead. We will change, and we will want to change . . . but we are afraid of what that change will bring.

While we were children, we hopefully had a routine, a consistency on which to base our lives. It doesn't have to be much. Dinner at six o'clock every night. The knowledge that every member of the family will be sitting there, even though they argue. Complaining about mom's cooking . . . these little things, we need. We need a consistency on which to fall back. Our little family unit.

We are now branching off into our own confusing worlds, our own significant thoughts, feelings, and uncertainties. We now imagine ourselves as one, sometimes lonely, unit. And it scares us.

We will continue to be frightened as adults, but there is a difference in the two. As an adult, I have gathered many experiences and have placed them inside of me. I will go on to use these experiences in my decision-making process. I will be able to judge the potential of a situation on previous information. And I can best act accordingly. But what is the adolescent to do? How does he base his decisions? He cannot draw from past experience. He must venture into the unknown and must be open to trial and error. He might make a mistake.

What is a mistake? If we don't hurt another person, where then is the mistake? There are none. Mistakes do not even exist. Oh, we may wish we would have done something differently. God knows, I curse myself out on not getting in on that stock that began at a dollar. It has now split and is at $40. I could have been RICH! I could have been rich if I hadn't made that mistake. Oh . . . I know there are some of you out there who really do think I made a mistake. You wish it had been you who would have known about that dollar stock. Did you make a mistake then? No, neither of us made a mistake.

How on earth can we learn if we don't make a (I don't even like to use the word) . . . take a risk? Life is a risk. Being on this earth is a risk. Do we then choose not to take a risk, and in turn, cease to be? Let your children make mistakes. Let them take a risk, using their values, the values you have taught them. Or even more important, what they have taught themselves. Mistakes, can almost always be fixed. It is our job as parents to teach them how to fix their mistakes without yelling at them in the process. It is our job to "cover" them, not necessarily protect them, they must feel the pain, but we must be there and support them in every way.

ANGER

March together
children of the past.
Your time is so long overdue.

Your mothers . . . your fathers
Force you   to grasp
soft, uncalloused hands
as they sit back   and laugh
at your latest phase.

But soon   so very soon
We ignorant children
shall cease our merriment
and our games shall be reality.

Our carefree, swinging hands
will melt into broken fists
and we will be a chain linked together
our links the colors of the rainbow.

Then you will stop   and finally see
Is that a black, a white, a yellow or red?
You will not even recognize us in our fury;
We will be united into one.

Only one stereotype among us,
that of a man   a human being.
Our chains and links so powerful
Not even you   of our once white blood
Can break.

(16 years old)

Ah . . . I think I see anger. We are angry about many things during these years. Anger is a very personal emotion, and it affects every single one of us differently. Maybe you're thinking I had a touch of PMS while I wrote that. It goes deeper than PMS. Our anger at this age is in our hearts.

> *"Satisfaction guaranteed!"*
> *The words ring out*
> *A new baby is born*
> *The words are bound*
> *To his delicate foot.*
> *What chance has he?*
> *What chance?*
>
> *You look at his color for your answer.*
> *You search for his wealth*
> *His material being.*
>
> *Life: Satisfaction guaranteed!*
>
> *The baby's eyes are stung*
> *by the grey sky.*
> *His mouth burns*
> *from impure waters.*
> *His lips are parched*
> *because of its scarcity.*
>
> *"Satisfaction guaranteed!"*
> *What chance has he?*
> *None.*
> *None to be a human being.*
>
> *(16 years old)*

Arguments can be good. Different viewpoints can be great. So what if someone thinks differently than you do? Opposing viewpoints bring answers to problems. They can bring answers to cancers. You should expect your children to have a different viewpoint. You should appreciate the way they question life.

My father was a compassionate man, but you know, it really didn't matter what I thought. He's one of the best fathers a person could have. But as a teenager, I had my views. They were very strong views, as most of ours are during this time. All I ever wanted was for him to take it to heart. To take my reasoning seriously. It didn't matter if it was right or wrong. All that mattered was that it would matter. I was a person with a brain too. Could there be a chance, some small chance I would know something that he, or another adult didn't?

It is an invisible wall we construct. We place it between our children and ourselves. As adults, we don't even know it is there. But our children do. They can see right throught it. And what do they see on the other side of that wall? Us. The enemy who doesn't want to listen.

Our children are all so precious. Each one of them has something to offer. But when they hold out their hands with their gifts to the world . . . we slap them. They don't know why . . . because they are still young. The ironic thing is that they could have grown in the meantime. They could have been working on whatever it was that was so special. And if their hands are slapped often enough, yes, they will forget what that special thing even was.

Can the adolescent survive? We can make it mighty tough. That little light grows dimmer as each year surfaces. Time, is not on their side, it is on ours. Remember, every minute of the day is very long to them. When we punish them with cutting glances for two days, those two days will be two hundred for them. It can be a long time to endure.

As adolescents, they have a right to be angry about a lot of things. Unfortunately, they haven't learned yet how to direct their anger. They spit it out at the person closest to them. Why? Because hopefully, we're there. They care about us. We are the people they love. Does this seem crazy? Why should it? Husbands and wives do it all the time. They love each other. Our children want the person or people they love to know what they think about things. They need to have dialogue in order to figure it out. And you know what? Their IQ is probably the same as ours. Isn't that amazing? They inherited our intelligence. They are just as smart as we are, only there is still a lot left for them to discover.

Their view of the world is just beginning to be formed. They only know what we have allowed them to know. Now it is their turn to find out for themselves. They must question. They must understand how or why people such as ourselves could even allow a war to happen. And they have this love inside of them, but they see people sleeping in cars and on the cement; mothers laying their babies down to sleep in gutters so they can try to make enough money to feed them the next day. They have to question, and they have to try out their voices. Our children must practice for what lies ahead. If they don't question, if they don't argue . . . how will anybody find the answers?

Arguing. Anger. Who would have thought our plump, giggling babies would argue with us? We took them to the doctor for every ear infection. We stayed up night after night watching them breath. We kept them alive.

We had it all planned, didn't we? Life would be perfect if we extended ourselves; a part of us would live on in our children. Only we missed one thing. They may look like us, but they are not us. They are unique.

Sometimes we may feel disappointment. And oh, we will certainly feel the frustration. But the word is "convenient." Life, once we have a child, is no longer convenient. It is a lot of hard work, and it gets harder each year.

Stick to the point when you argue. Pinpoint what the problem really is. It makes no sense at all to argue about personalities or what happened two years ago when you're discussing a curfew for the basketball game. But we do it all the time.

SUMMARY

By now we realize we have many feelings and emotions erupting inside of us during this period of life called adolescence. Our bodies at the same time are producing hormones. This, coupled with our sudden awareness of feelings, makes for a complex human being. (We will look at our bodily changes during chapter seven.)

I am convinced our senses are at their peak during adolescence. As we grow older they seem to grow dimmer, because we learn to mold ourselves into society. In comprehending the growing process, we must look back and understand our infants. Our infants acted barbaric. If they were any bigger . . . they would have killed us. As parents, we spent most of our time teaching them how to control their bodies. Then, when they were young children, our concerns were that of blending them into a social atmosphere. We insisted they get along with other humans. So, by the time they reach adolescence, there really has not been a whole lot of time that has elapsed. And we expect them to be perfect, able to fend for themselves, but not to question.

In the first edition of this book I used the example of Dr. Spock in Star Trek to emphasize society's lack of showing emotions. Our dear Dr. Spock has, in the meantime, learned something. That it is okay to cry. It is okay to cry. But more importantly, when we let our adolescents know it is okay to cry, we must communicate and understand their pain.

CHAPTER TWO

Free To Be

*P*EER CONTACT, PEER pressure and friendship are strong influences within the adolescent years. I do not like to link peer contacts, their pressures, and friendships together in one section, since I do feel there is a difference among the three. However, they are usually thought of as being one and the same, so they will appear together.

During this chapter we will discuss specific experiences and situations, because I feel these details may help us understand. I also feel we will have to pin an age on adolescence in order not to be vague. For myself, I see adolescence beginning at the age of 11 following through age 17 for the girls and 18 for the boys. The growing process then rapidly leads us into young adulthood. Ten years ago I would have said adolescence begins at ages 13 or 14, but as the world gets more sophisticated, so do our children. In some situations, adolescence may be beginning at the ages of 8, 9, or 10. (My own daughter may be entering adolescence at the age of 7.)

Peer contacts, peer pressures, and friendships are a combination of two unrelated aspects. Peer contacts and peer pressures may change daily, whereas friendship is something that continues to grow.

THE SENSITIVE ADOLESCENT

In regard to peer pressure, I must have run the gamut. I was the kid everyone plotted to pick on, bully or want to physically fight. Looking back I would have to say I was placed in this position because I was vulnerable to it. Like most of us. They knew I cared.

There will be many times when the sensitive adolescent will be afraid to say "no" just because he or she is sensitive. When feelings are hurt they run at different levels in each one of us. We may think it is easier to say "yes," than to be ridiculed . . . again.

19

When someone shoved that first cigarette in my face, I didn't want it. But I took it so they wouldn't laugh at me. It made me choke. My eyes watered. But then, it was only one cigarette.

They let me get by with puffing it for only so long. Then I had to prove myself worthy of their attention by inhaling. I choked again.

Then it wasn't just one cigarette, I had to carry a pack around with me so they would know I was serious. I did become serious. I became hooked on them. I took that first cigarette when I was 15 years old. I am now 32 and still smoking. That first cigarette grew into a habit I can't break, and I know it will kill me. If I ran into that person today who put that cigarette in my mouth . . . I would punch them. But then, it was my fault, wasn't it?

The bullies never pick on the kid who could not care less. They aim sharpened arrows for the child to whom they will do the most damage: the sensitive adolescent. If you are a sensitive adolescent, it will be harder for you to say "no" than for anyone else. The pain you carry inside is unique, and others will have a very hard time understanding it. Whereas other people can throw certain remarks to the wind and let them fly, it settles inside of you. It sinks into the core of you. And you will smile, won't you? And pretend it doesn't hurt.

This sensitivity, which usually announces itself as pain, is hard to live with. When other adolescents are feeling all alone, you are feeling a hundred times worse. That's because whatever it is has not attacked just a portion of you, it has ripped apart your entire being.

This pain will make you stronger, but it will take years before you can acknowledge it as an asset. This happens to be a very special pain, and there is a reason you must feel it. You must keep your head up high and overcome each obstacle as it comes. You will be learning in the process, learning in ways others never will. There WILL come a day . . . when you will shine brighter than anybody.

And the bullies? The bullies nine times out of ten turn out to be losers. Losers in ways you can't even imagine, because they never took the time to understand or to care. We must not hate them, we must try to understand them. There is something very much missing in their lives, something that we will probably never know. But that's okay, as long as we can realize their actions are really not directed toward us . . . they are directed toward themselves.

ADOLESCENT HARASSMENT

This will be a fun one. (You see, I can laugh about it now.) There were so many times. I can remember sitting on the front lawn of the junior high waiting for the bus. I wasn't yet one of the cool kids, because I didn't know how to French kiss. And my parents wouldn't let me go to all night parties.

One of the cool girls came up to me and called me a squirrel. At the time I had three squirrels as pets. I thought they were really neat little creatures. I spent hours with them; feeding them, they'd sit on my knee, they'd join me in my favorite tree. I thanked her for the compliment. In fact, I thanked everyone for a whole week before I realized, that no, this was not a compliment, and I had better learn how to French kiss. But wait a minute. I didn't want to kiss anybody. So why should I? I was the "squirrel" for the remainder of the school year until everybody went home for summer vacation. Of course, I dwelled on it for the entire summer and insisted my parents move to another state.

Let's put it this way. We never know why people like to pick on us. Maybe they picked on me because I was a late starter in wearing nylons. The first time was in the fifth grade when we went to the state capitol. I wore red bell-bottomed pants, and the nylons had a gigantic run through the center. Maybe they never forgot the incident.

My body was pretty normal for that age. I was beginning to get zits just like everybody else. But one of my friends (yes, we call them friends even though they are enemies), had this thing about bending my fingers backward. Actually, she didn't want to bend my fingers, she wanted to break them. But God had smiled upon me once again, that's because God had given me double-jointed fingers. You can bend them all day long! They can even bend in different directions at the same time. Boy, was she surprised! She thought she had actually broken them. She thought I was so brave for not crying that she was even nice to me once after that.

Adolescents come under many headings during this period of life. A few names they will answer to are: zit face, retard, palsy, tinsel teeth, fatso, major mac attack, etc. You can project any name you want. If the flaw fits . . . you gotta wear it. I personally bore the name of "Hairy" at the age of twelve.

My nickname came about because I am a brunette, and the hair on my arms and legs was naturally dark. I also had a little mustache. I can remember not wanting to get within a mile of anyone. I would have given anything to have had braces.

And so, my unsightly hair, although it really wasn't all THAT bad, was even more apparent than if I had been a blonde bombshell (which I finally tried at the age of 30 because you can do anything you want to when you're that old). Naturally, I was devastated and vowed never to return to school again.

My parents were beside themselves, and we all set forth on a journey to come to some sort of rapid solution regarding this most recent catastrophe. Besides, my father, in his own sweet manner, insisted I finish school. What could I do? Should it be bleached or should it be removed? This was the discussion at the dinner table for a week. It could be bleached, but then the kids might really make fun of me. "Give me a break!" I cried.

The final outcome was that the hair on the legs had to go. Mind you, it was not as if I were a baby and was losing my first curls. The old razor was involved, and I was the one who got to use it.

The armpits and the hair on my forearms were a different story. Armpits are never seen at that age unless it is summer. It wasn't summer, so the pits had to wait. As for the hair on the forearms, the decision was left up to me. And I would have to live the rest of my life . . . with that decision. I wanted to rip it off by my teeth, but they wouldn't let me. I decided to accept it as a part of me. Things could have been worse they reminded me. I could have gone through life minus an arm or leg. I should be glad I HAD an arm to support hair growth.

The point is, it is even more devastating to return to school after a physical revelation such as this. Everybody knows you did SOME-THING because you are suddenly DIFFERENT. It only takes a second for them to figure it out. They knew they could no longer call me "Hairy." They would have to think of something else.

Do you know what else happens to us—as we're sitting there taking it on the chin, hoping we won't have to turn the other cheek? I was standing by my locker in 9th grade, trying not to be noticed. My name was now "Pancake" because I was flat chested. "Hey, find any buried treasure lately?" My locker partner showed up at my elbow. There was something different about her. She had braces! The words suddenly changed. The abuse changed. People walking by didn't talk about me, they talked about her. "Just a minute and I'll go get my metal detector." "Can we borrow your mouth for shop? We're getting into heavy metal."

Do you know what I felt? Could I feel compassion, warmth or sympathy? I don't like to admit it . . . I felt relief! Relief it wasn't ME. God forgive me, I hope I didn't smile.

So you see . . . sometimes we can't turn to one another, as peers, at that age. We need an adult to try to understand and explain adolescent harassment. We don't want to hear, "Oh, they'll forget about it in a week." "Oh, I'm sure they didn't mean it." You can bet your bottom dollar they meant it. Sometimes we won't tell our parents because we feel so embarrassed, or stupid for some reason. It's like we don't want to repeat the words out loud, that's how much they hurt us. When this happens to us we need someone to objectively view the situation and someone who can and does care what is happening to us.

SHOW AND TELL TIME

During adolescence we never really think of "Show and Tell." We think of "Show and Tell" belonging to five- and six-year-olds. And does it! Isn't it marvelous when we discover the difference? I locked a five-year-old in our garage—I was also five if you're wondering. I don't know how parents do it, but they always know when you're doing something you're not supposed to be doing. I heard a bang on the door. "Open the door."

"Gee, Mom, I was just looking. He didn't mind."

"Show and Tell" comes back to haunt us around the ages of 10, 11 and 12. It's an additional engagement, a rerun. A sequel like *Jaws 2*. Show and Tell 2. Usually it's the male species who thinks of it first. This is not to say girls will not find an interest too. It crops up in the form of a game. My first time happened in a garage. There were three of us. Two girls and a boy. The boy wanted us to get naked and dress in plastic bags. Good try . . . I didn't want to get naked. I wasn't old enough yet. I thought I might wait until I was 16. I ran home.

The second experience took place in a neighbor's yard. They had four big pine trees that were so big you could crawl underneath them like a fort. We usually used them as forts, but this was something special. They announced it throughout the neighborhood. So and so was going to take her clothes off. Who could miss that? We had a whole gang there by the time the word got out. No plastic bags this time, it was bare it all. Even the boys joined in. I had two brothers, so I wasn't surprised. I was surprised in seeing a female body. I was surprised that the boys were surprised. I chickened out again. Don't ask me why modesty is what it is.

The game of "Show and Tell" will be played whether we like it or not, so where is the answer? We must make sure our children are thoroughly educated. It may be done in innocence this time . . . but what about next time? They must know that maybe later on they will not be able to say no with a chuckle or a smile. We need to expose the potential danger for the future.

FADS

We will go through many fads in a lifetime, and the adolescent is certainly no exception. There is only one common thread between fads, and that is, they cost money. That's because they don't last.

During adolescence fads are important. They make us feel like we belong. I remember the day wearing white socks went out. I walked to school feeling like an idiot. How was my mother to understand I was suddenly an alien? I had a whole drawer filled with white socks. So you beg, you plead and you cry over it. But do they understand? No.

During the olden days our fads were wearing white lipstick, bell bottomed pants, jeans, clothes too big for us, looking sloppy, and dieting so that we looked like the fashion model, Twiggy. Twiggy probably had anorexia at the time, only we didn't know it.

Today we wear our father's underwear, color our hair purple and pierce our ears. Things haven't changed much. And what really hasn't changed is our need to look like everybody else. Things are hard enough at this age, but we have to look at both sides of the story. Parents don't like to spend money on fads, they think they're a waste of money. But then we have to look at fads from the viewpoint of the child. It's important to them, more important than you'll ever know. Make a compromise so that you're both happy. Then you can borrow each other's clothes.

MONEY CAN'T BUY YOU FRIENDS

An interesting observation on peer groups begins at a very early age. Human beings are attracted to the attractive. It doesn't matter whether you're an adult or a child. People love money, nice clothes, attractive houses, good food—the list goes on and on. Study a popular girl or boy sometime. Are they better dressed than their peers? Do their parents offer them things other children do not have? Are they in extra activities, and are their homes polished with treats and friendliness? Who says money can't buy you friends? Money can always buy you friends.

Money may not buy happiness, but it draws friends like honey draws a bee. These people are called "fair-weather friends." These are people who will be your friend when everything is going great. When you are on top, you can have all the friends you want. But when things start going down hill, parents get a divorce, you can't afford the nice clothes, you drop out of activities . . . you are poison, honey.

Look at all the rock stars who had everything. The movie stars. They had plenty of friends who hung around for all the good times. But when they were alone . . . they destroyed themselves. What can happen with teen-agers can be devastating. When parents provide adolescents with all the goodies, it is imperative values are locked in place. It is great to have friends (that is for sure); however, you must be certain it is not the money but YOU they like. Because, once these adolescents are on their own during 17 through 22, they aren't going to know who likes them for what. They may turn to sexual permissiveness. If we can't tell if people like us for who we are and the need for love exists (which it most certainly will) . . . we just may offer them our bodies as a compromise.

PUTTING ON THE GLOVES

A problem we can run into at the ages of 13 and 14 is other children wanting to fight us. It seems silly to me now, but boy, when I was 13, it was a pretty big deal. There are times when you can avoid these people, but there will be times when you can't.

Unfortunately, I am unable to place myself inside a boy's mind while this is happening. I can only speak from a girl's perspective. Maybe it's the same, the boys will have to let me know.

There was a girl when I was 13 who was in love with the boy who sat in front of me. (I'll call her Mary.) Mary thought I was in love with him because I yelled at him every time he bothered me. She sent out notes to the entire classroom telling them I was stealing her boyfriend away from her. They sympathized with her!

Here we will pause to identify the major form of communication during adolescence. Notes. And do we gossip? Whew! There goes not one stone unturned by the end of the day. Everything is known about everybody. These messages are folded into a million pieces. They are turned into works of art. And any one of us could make a living as a spy the way we can sneak it past the teacher. But if the teacher catches you? The note is read aloud to the entire classroom. It doesn't matter what's on it. Your soul is hung out to dry. Apparently, they do not know the words or the meaning of the Privacy Act.

Okay, so back to Mary. Round one. Mary, by the end of the day had everybody hating my guts. I was shunned. An outcast. You would have thought I had herpes. Then Mary took it a step further. She wanted to fight. Not only was the one classroom involved by the end of the week, we had three whole grades placing bets on who would win.

Scared, was I scared? Physically fight? I decided to have a talk with good old Mary. We had never talked before. See how good communication works? I told her I didn't LIKE her boyfriend, let alone LOVE him. This did not satisfy her. She still wanted to fight. After all, how could she turn back now? It was her honor at stake.

I'll never forget the big day—the day of the big fight. I was surprised they didn't announce it over the loudspeaker. Some kids brought refreshments from home. I never told my parents about it—their daughter, walking into the lions den to be maimed for life, or even worse . . . killed.

No, it wasn't like you see in the movies. Nobody taught me how to punch like Mohammed Ali, or the basic techniques of karate. And I wasn't Rambo, where I could just throw a grenade in her face and be done with it. I was just a girl with no friends by her side not knowing what to do.

I think she was scared too. A whole flock of people surrounded her as she walked down the block. I had always walked on the other side. I didn't that day. It's called meeting them on their own territory. I followed behind all by myself. Even our future homecoming queen was up with the rest of them. Miss humanitarian. Then Mary stopped. I was forced to approach her.

I drew up every ounce of strength I had. I didn't have a muscle to speak of—I found the strength in my gut. Actually, I asked God to please put something clever in my mouth. I gave her the look mothers give their children when they've done something wrong. It's called the "look that could kill." I spoke up in a nasally tone of voice. (I have always been very sarcastic.) And I shook my head at her. (It's the shake you give someone when they've done something utterly stupid—like you can't believe anybody could be that dumb.) "Sorry . . . I don't fight."

She gave me a look back, as if I were chicken. I said, "Why should I risk my face over this?" What could she say? I had given the impression it was beneath me. She was now the fool.

Mary continued to hate my guts for the next six years. There were times when we ran into each other, but I ignored her. Ignoring people REALLY gets to them. Little did she know I was dying inside. I asked someone about her years later. They told me she was stripping in a lingerie bar. It made me stop following her progress.

Fighting with words is always better than fighting with fists. It indicates you're smarter than they are, and it gives you the edge. They may think we're strange, and they may punch us out anyway, but what if it works?

People like to fight us for the sake of competition, or the sake of frustration. If they're not good in anything, they can always put a fist in our face. You have been challenged to a dual, you have been challenged of your integrity . . . so challenge them back. It takes more than brawn in this world, it takes brains. Figure out what YOU are good at, and make them conform to YOU. You're smart . . . you'll figure it out.

CLIQUES (OR SPECIAL PEER GROUPS)

Clique (klik) n. a small exclusive group of people.
Ain't it the truth? Exclusive unto themselves. (A personal observation.) There is no way of getting around cliques, for they certainly do exist. Cliques can be good or bad—probably both. It is very important to be accepted as one of the group. Traveling through the ages between 12 and 18, adolescents usually belong to more than one group as they discover new interests. During the ages of 12 through 14 or 15, the common bond between peers is distance. We get about as far as our bicycles or walking will take us. We go to the nearest penny arcade, our favorite street corner, local park, or patch of land. This is not to say we can't travel across town on our bicycles. My girlfriend and I had boyfriends who rode their bikes 10 miles to see us.

We talk about our newest love, play video games, make-out at the movies, smoke cigarettes, eat pizzas, and drink diet soda. Or, we smoke dope, sneak a bottle out of our parent's liquor cabinet, have sex, or get high on a bottle of hair spray or our mother's styling mousse. (We'll go into the second portion of this paragraph in our drug chapter.)

During the ages of 16, 17 and 18, we see a definite change. Chances are, the people we knew earlier, we no longer even associate with. Basically because we can now drive cars or take the bus.

There are two sets of peer groups during this age. Now I get to spill the beans. We must be fair to both sides. There are the kids who "do" and the kids who "don't." They simply do not mix. Not anymore. There is only one exception. The kids who "don't" may be sexually active. (You know those hormones, it's hard to say no.)

And parents . . . you will never know. Kids can talk their way in and out of anything. I used to skip school and go to demonstrations against the war. I hadn't been in class for three days. I was out getting maced. My band teacher finally pulled me out of another class and met me in front of the principal's office. He wanted to know where I had been. I first began explaining I simply hadn't felt like going to class. I was tired of playing the flute. Of course he didn't buy it. So then, you think of something to which they can't even respond. I told him I thought I was pregnant and had to get it checked out. Of course I couldn't have told my parents. I hadn't even had sex! He thought I was acting responsibly. Everything was fine. My parents never found out, and I didn't get detention.

I went to another demonstration (or maybe it was a lake because the weather was nice). Only this time I skipped out of Social Studies. We had a project that would have taken a month to complete. I didn't have it done. I couldn't even relate to the subject. I wrote a paper on the importance of Americans standing up for what they believed. My argument was, "Isn't that what Social Studies is all about?" I was putting it to practical use. What could he say? I got an A for the course. Everybody else received C's and D's on their assignments because it hadn't made sense anyway.

There is a separation occurring in schools today. Years ago they may have been able to mix, but not anymore. The kids who "do" are doing drugs, are sexually active, and are truant to a certain degree. The kids who "don't" base their life styles on traveling in groups, being active in athletics, music, drama, etc. Each of these groups will put the other down. They will not be able to relate to each other.

Of course, as a parent we all wish our children were in peer groups who didn't. Five years ago I wrote it didn't have to be looked upon in a negative fashion. That kids could experiment and come out just fine. There will be exceptions, but there will also be times when we just can't know.

When I was in high school I traveled in both peer groups. I had friends who "didn't." They were cheerleaders and athletes, debaters and chess players, school photographers and writers. They are now publishers, editors, ministers, doctors, scientists, international fashion models, attorneys, actors and actresses, and heads of multimillion dollar companies. And to bring the point a little closer to home on what can happen to us down the road, one of my friends went to high school with Jessica Lange. My friend said, "She didn't stand out in the crowd. She was just average, virtually unnoticeable."

Then there were the friends who "did." We can never really know exactly where it will lead. It may take years to catch up with us. This is what we must remember. We can read about it, people can try to tell us, but we don't believe them. Why should we? Believe me, we just don't know.

One of my friends was found strangled to death in a hotel room in Las Vegas. He was killed with a necktie by a man and a woman during a coke deal. The casket remained closed for the funeral because his face was so distorted.

The minister said, "He had lived in the fast lane," but he didn't elaborate. We all knew, all of us standing around the casket at the burial site knew, he had been spacing out on drugs ever since he had been 15. We knew there was a chance drugs could kill him, we just never thought they would kill him like this.

I stood across from his mother and tears streamed down my face. Putting a friend in the ground is like nothing else. Especially when they didn't have to die. Yes, he did have a lot to offer the world . . . only the world never knew it.

And I have loved many people in my life. I saw one of them on TV a few months ago. It's always fun seeing people you know on TV. But this wasn't. It was a mug shot taken while he was being booked for murder.

The time we had spent together when I was 16 and 17 were good times. We laughed and we loved everything about the world. He smoked dope then, and I didn't really think anything of it. A lot of people smoked dope. He even did a little coke once in a while, but that was alright. People are allowed their freedom, we didn't know it was psychologically addicting and that it could kill you. All we knew was that it was a drug that probably came from South America.

I touched base with him a few years back. Things were good. Or so it seemed. I was working on a book regarding chemical agents in the Orient. He was traveling back and forth doing documentaries on Agent Orange and dioxins left behind in Vietnam and Cambodia. We even talked of combining our two subjects. He said he had been on national TV with his findings. I was actually jealous because he was doing something to benefit the world. What had I contributed?

We never really do know. We can believe in our friends, but we can never know. I read about his case briefly in the newspaper. It said his roommate had been shot in the back of the head. It was winter, and the body had been hidden in a garage for two months. My friend was also being accused of using money from the dead man's bank account and his car. The article also mentioned cocaine. It lead me to suspect the use of cocaine was not done in innocence. This was crime to its highest degree.

I had loved him. I had loved him a lot. I felt sick for five days after reading the newspaper article, and I felt total shock when his face appeared on TV with a number under it. I ran things over and over in my mind. I thought back to the good times we had. Then I got this picture in my mind of a young man being murdered in cold blood – not in self-defense. I imagined the victim kneeling with a gun to the back of his head like in pictures you see when someone is being assasinated in another country. The victim was probably not given a blindfold. He probably knew exactly what was going on until the end. It was no longer child's play. It was the real world. And the question will never be answered . . . WHY? But we do know the answer, don't we? It was because of addiction and money.

Friends can be, never what they appear to be. We can do just fine, but sometimes we can't. Many of the girls having sex during high school became pregnant shortly thereafter. They married the men who made them pregnant. Now they look for the checks to come every month either from the husbands who left them or from welfare.

During the years between 17 and 21 we travel through a difficult situation. We go away to college or to work, or maybe we stay and our peer group moves away. We can have a hard time adjusting. We no longer have the security of being with our peer group, and we are still adolescents at 17. We may choose to enter a new peer group. This may come in the form of a fraternity or a sorority or a new work situation.

When we join new peer groups, we will probably find differences from our past peer groups. These are not people whom we have known or have grown up with. There are new likes and dislikes or new ideas of what fun itself is all about. (Like maybe you don't like to chug beer until you throw up.) In the past we may have been totally accepted, but now we run into the problem of people not liking us and of us not liking them.

One of the hardest things to accept or to understand is that everybody does not have to like us. But it's okay! It's a new learning experience we must face in order to grow effectively.

Difficulties may arise in these new situations. You know what happens when you attend a new college or a new job? You run into the same people all the time. It's like living in a small town. So what can you do to make things easier? Stick to your studying, do a better job at work, get fabulous grades or brownie points with the boss. Things CAN turn themselves around. Time has a way of taking care of everything. However, we must see to it our meantime is put to work in a good, positive manner. Or we can conform. But who wants to conform, anyway? It's so much fun being different!

OUR ABILITY TO CONTROL OTHERS

There is a problem that can crop up once in awhile, but there is a simple solution. Now that we are in our teens, we have, hopefully, justly proven ourselves worthy of trust. Our parents can leave us for short or long periods of time while they run off to discover who they are once again. (Adults change too, and we must keep up with one another.)

Where the problem lies, is when the adolescent is left all by himself with total responsibility. This is one of the most important things we can do for our children. If you think caring for them and showing them we love them is important for their self-esteem, just try trusting them. But what can happen quicker than lightning?

It's PARTY TIME!! Being an adolescent and being left by ourselves is very tempting. We have the whole house to ourselves, hmmmm, let's see what we can pack into an evening or overnight. First you call your best friend. "The coast is clear . . . wanna party?" Of course they want to party, only they'll have to call just one other person — just to make them jealous. The adolescent agrees, reluctantly. They sense a problem, but it is not a problem yet.

So you sit anxiously awaiting your friend. The problem rings the doorbell. Your problem is now in the range of fifty kids.

We are not responsible for others' actions. But if forced to, we will try to control their actions. It happens to adults. As an adult I have difficulty in controlling a large crowd. People will do what they want to do, you just have to hope they do it within reason.

We must not expect adolescents to have the ability to control others' actions. They're working very hard on controlling their own actions. Things happen. Things happen, and there will be times when we have no control. The parent and adolescent must sit down and discuss the possibilities of what can go wrong. The adolescent doesn't know unless you explain it to him. And then, if you haven't discussed it, and something happens, you will probably blame him. You'll give him the old "I can't trust you anymore. Okay, kiddo, now you're REALLY going to have to prove yourself." Which, in all likelihood will take the next 30 years. SO WHY BOTHER?

Sit down and discuss it. Discuss who is welcome in your home. You are not dealing with reality if you think your adolescent is going to sit home by himself. Give him one or two people. Then the adolescent lets the friends know that he will kill them if they open their mouths. Tape their mouths shut if you have to. Simply, "DON'T TELL ANYONE YOU ARE ALONE." It will work every time. Mom and Dad will then return to a calm, quiet, and peaceful household, and sure as shootin' they'll plan the next weekend away from you.

VIDEO GAMES

I have mixed emotions on video games. We live in the computer age and we must expect contact in regard to this aspect. When I began this book, I told you I had certain opinions. This is one to be taken as that. Just an opinion. Let me just try here, to look objectively at this. The good points as I see them: 1) It's a game. 2) People have fun. 3) It probably builds manual dexterity. 4) It may increase quicker brain response. 5) A number of movies came out with kids playing video games who ended up saving the world by using something similar to that of a video game. Some would call it sensationalism. 6) It gives people something to do, a place to meet their friends. 7) Final good point: It's a gigantic industry. Someone makes a ton of money. Where does your money go? Is five minutes of play worth a quarter? That's $3.00 an hour. A mere pittance in anyone's book. One must then make almost the minimum wage to come out even. I guess it's a question of how much money one makes in a week. Of course, that also means two cokes an hour at 50 cents each, so that makes it $4.00 an hour, which means one must make $5.00 an hour to come out even. This is calculated on the cheaper games, like the ones in the entrance of a drug store. You'd have to throw in transportation. That's worth (what would that be worth?) probably $4.00 even if your parents drove you, not taking into consideration they usually (middle income) make $12.00 an hour when they're actually working, and it takes at least an hour to transport you. (Actually, it would be about the same if you took your own car; gas, maintenance, insurance, stains on the seats, etc.). So, as I do when I always estimate, we'll look at the larger figure. Three hours of play cost you (this is what it's costing SOMEONE): almost $20 (which in all actuality is $30 for tax purposes). Oh, I forgot. Five bucks at (we won't say where, some hamburger joint) which makes it $25 and $35 for tax purposes. If one does this twice a week, that's $50 and $70.

A few negative points: 1) It's hard to carry on a conversation with someone who's playing. You're going to tell me they're concentrating. This is all fine if you came with someone you didn't want to talk to anyway. 2) People have experienced epileptic seizures during play. 3) People have been known to steal in order to play. 4) When video games are not located in a bar, the adolescent will most likely find the games located in a penny arcade. Everybody's safe, right? Your friends are there, you can protect yourself. I know I could, and I was really resourceful as a kid. But there are other people besides your friends and players who hang around to watch. You may find your local pimp, sex offender, or kidnapper. The cost of a child in this day and age is $50–100. It's hard to say why or how people disappear from anywhere. One minute they're here . . . the next minute they're gone. They probably went to the bathroom, right? Sure, via a van waiting outside. Many people do find New York or L.A. an exciting place to visit. I do. I just wouldn't like to live there unexpectedly strapped to a bed with a cattle prod convincing me to cooperate. Oh, I forgot again. There are also people who like to sell you drugs.

As a parent, what happened to responsibility? We have the ability to be just as exciting as punching a button! You know what the secret ingredient is? Interest. Interest in what our children are interested in.

Or, you may not even know WHAT your children are talking about. Chances are, it's true. But, OH, do they love to explain it to you? Sometimes it is irritating to learn you don't know everything. Especially when it's from someone younger. A KID, at that. Who knows the answer. Boy, it sure is hard to be careful . . . to not learn something you really didn't want to know. Double negative turns into a positive . . . GOTTCHA!

LIMITS

In the earlier edition of this book, I wrote: "As adolescents, our children need and want limits set for them. In some ways they cry out for your love, understanding, and attention. And perhaps when the situation arises, when they find it hard to say, 'No,' because everyone's doing it . . . what better excuse than to say, 'My parents would KILL me if they ever found out!' Let's offer them this excuse on an UNDERSTANDING LEVEL."

I still believe this, but I have to add to it. I had a partner in business once. It was practically unbelievable the way she ran her life. There was a passion which surpassed anything I could imagine. Our families always came first. We delighted in the interruptions of the day. That's because the interruptions were always from our families. We would smile at each other, each knowing, what was important. Who else would have understood, what we knew our smiles really meant?

I went through a few of the teen years with her, with her two boys, and I loved it. How could anything turn out so right? The woman worked until two in the morning. I have seen her drained, and I have seen her drag herself to the door—ready to debate any philosophy of life. I don't know how she did it.

I had a conversation with her the other day. We had each branched off on our own and made money. But things were the same. We started talking about what was important. Her first questions were of Jessica. She wanted to know where her brain was, at this point in her life. Then we began discussing school systems and how they dealt with minds academically. After dissecting the topic, I started to think Jessica and I were both just drifting through the kindergarten year. I explained I was at home writing. Then I apologized. I'm so used to apologizing for being at home. I forgot I was talking to someone who knew the difference. She laughed. I had forgotten how much I had missed her. We could have both made as much money as we wanted to—it was a matter of choice, not a cop-out. It's not that we don't like money, we LOVE money. But we knew, if you didn't have a happy, orderly home, nothing else mattered.

In two hours we talked about 15 subjects. What was ironic was she began to tell me about people who were calling her. People wanted to know what she had done right. How had she raised two boys who turned out the way they did? I told her she should write a book. She talked about simple points while they were growing up: 1) She always told them how smart they were. It started at age two. 2) They never had to question their intelligence or talents, it was understood. 3) If they did not understand their intelligence, it was their problem. SHE knew how smart they were. 4) They each had something very special about themselves. If the opposite was ever expressed, it wasn't tolerated. It was their job to learn as much as they could. It would be their fault if they didn't live up to their potential.

The topic of the day was always open at the dinner table. They proposed a new topic every night. It could be a new breed of dog, it didn't matter. They would reach for a book and learn about it. Nobody knew everything, it was the "You can find out if you want to" attitude.

5) Limits were set. The most important thing was that you followed through. THE KIDS KNEW THE EXACT PUNISHMENT FOR EACH VIOLATION. She said, "You cry into your pillow at night by yourself because it kills you inside." One of the children was asked by a peer, "So, you think you're pretty smart, don't you? Why are you so smart? And why do you get good grades?" At the age of 11 his answer was, "Because my mom expects me to get A's. If she didn't think I could get A's, she wouldn't expect me to. Besides, she'd KILL me if I didn't."

This in turn, spurred another discussion, on talent. My friend happens to be a math whiz. She recalled an instance in college when she was struggling with a course. She brought the problems to her brother who was even more of a math whiz. They sat and went through problem after problem. He finally looked at her and said, "Don't you see this?" She replied, "No."

He looked at her straight in the eye. "You know how smart you are, and I know how smart you are . . . but there's something you have to face. You have gone as far as you can go in this area."

The point is, we all have to recognize our talents. We have to go after those talents and take them as far as we can. And sometimes, we concentrate on only that one talent. There are MANY talents in each one of us. We have to discover what those other ones are too, and then go after them!

My dear friend had taught me another lesson in life. We got back to our motherhood. She began to laugh. It had been about when the boys were 16 and 18 and her husband decided he should be the one to take care of the discipline. The boys couldn't figure out WHAT was going on and were very confused. She had to say, "But it's all done! The discipline is all done! I started when they were one-year-old! We have a couple of great kids . . . they KNOW what is right and what is wrong! Now we get to ENJOY them . . . we get to reap the reward! Yes, you can thank me . . . it wasn't easy."

This mother had instilled in them that they had so much to offer, so much to learn, that it WOULD be their fault if they failed. She had given all she could. The boys knew it, this is what is so important. She had loved them. She had listened to them. She had taught them everything she knew. She had sacrificed. She had disciplined them. She had cried with them and understood their pain.

Then it was kind of cute. Here she had talked about all of this, and it had been so inspirational . . . if you work hard enough and love hard enough, you'll end up with really neat kids. Then she said, "Of course (she said this slowly), they KNEW . . . if they had done it any DIFFERENTLY, . . . I would have KILLED them."

My eyebrows shot up. It was the way she had said it. *I* thought she meant it. She paused at the other end. "They really thought I meant it." No kidding. "It's all in the WAY you say it, you have to MEAN it."

Then she added in disbelief (I was still trying to catch my breath), "Nobody follows through! Parents let their kids get away with everything. Then they turn around and give them anything they want. Then the parents wonder WHY, when they finally discipline once or twice, why all of a sudden it doesn't work. Do they think it's supposed to be magic or something? You have to MEAN what you say ALL OF THE TIME. You have to be CONSISTENT." She laughed again. I choked. It had been just yesterday. I had threatened Jessica. I hadn't followed through because I didn't want to take the time. It wasn't convenient. I didn't want to get emotionally involved. I had too much to do. Besides, if I took 15 minutes out to punish her, that would have been MY 15 minutes when I could have been doing something else. I had let it slide.

"They were always responsible kids," she said, going on. "I'd give them a curfew, and they'd follow it. They KNEW they were old enough to tell time. And if they weren't smart enough to tell time, they couldn't go out. I'm not going to give someone MY car if they can't figure out what time it is or locate a phone. I would be the one who was crazy."

"They came in at midnight or one in the morning. They always knew I'd be up, and if I wasn't, they'd wake me. They always gave me a hug and a kiss and they would plop down to talk. That was our special time together. They could talk about anything. They always knew they had an extra hour, it didn't matter what time it was, they knew they could talk to me until dawn."

We talked a while longer. She never shut me off either. If I wanted to talk, I could talk. Or listen. She was always a person I could listen to . . . that's because she always meant what she said.

"Both of them are continuing school . . . I'd rather he went to a different school . . . our political views are different now, it's really strange . . ."

I interjected, "But that's alright . . ."

"NO, IT'S NOT," she replied horrified. "I worked very HARD instilling my views in them, they're smart boys, they'll come around."

They probably will.

Set limits so your children know the rules of the game. Let them know the exact punishment for each offense. We have to love and understand them, but we have a real responsibility to set those limits.

PEER CONTACTS AND PEER PRESSURE SUMMARY

When I wrote this book five years ago a word kept popping up. Sometimes I called it by it's name, and other times I didn't. It popped up in practically every single subject we discussed. Maybe it was because I liked the word so much, but as it turned out, the little word became the answer to practically everything. It was *self-esteem*.

It had to do with belief—in the little light that shines within. It starts as an ember and we keep feeding it until it burns. Burns until it has enough light and life to shine all over the world.

It is SO easy to put out. All we have to do is put our hand over it. I had two children in the house. I usually have five. My house—I will live and probably die by this (it probably will kill me, but I'll die happy)—is always open. I was irritated because two six-year-olds weren't moving fast enough for me. We had to get lunch in, get dressed for school, catch the bus . . ."Get your coat on," I barked. That's because they were messing around. It's important that children mess around, it makes life fun . . . that is until it is inconvenient for us.

They looked at me in shock. They looked at each other in shock. They wanted to discuss it between themselves. Did I feel like a jerk? Yes.

Jessica asked, "Do you know what you just said?"

"Yes, I said get your coat on." I had softened my voice. I was trying to pretend they weren't smart enough to catch the change.

"It was your voice," she said. She had to grope for a word. "It was . . . rude."

I looked into their faces. To these two little people who loved so much, who played so hard, and had so much to try to learn. I could have disappeared. Looking up to me as an adult. One who knows. She should have said, "Shame on you." But shame is not a word she knows.

We always believe in our parents. It's something that goes without saying. You soften your voice, you put care in your words, and you say, "I'm sorry. I should have known better . . . please forgive me." Then they put their arms around you and tell you "I love you."

Peer contacts and peer pressures affect every single one of us on a different level. We can pick our group. It's up to us. I am not here to influence. All I can do is explain my own experiences. It doesn't mean my experiences were either good or bad, they just were. They were just things that happened in one life.

I will say, however, it is EXTREMELY difficult to travel between one or the other. You will have to choose. I just happen to be one of the lucky ones who got away with it.

Just remember, parents, you can use all the positive reinforcement you want, but if you don't actually love them and SHOW them you love them AT LEAST ten times a day AND discipline them . . . it's not going to work. Your child can read you like a book. And you, as a parent, can read all the books you want . . . but having the knowledge does NOTHING unless you put it to PRACTICAL use.

FRIENDSHIP

During adolescence, friendship blossoms into something very special. We find a certain closeness, a common bond, and a very special love for someone other than ourselves—someone we can call our "friend." During the years of 12 through 16, it is usually a member of the same sex.

We run the gamut of feelings with this person or persons, and when we have these feelings, there is the possibility of getting hurt. Because we love them so much, they can hurt us. If we didn't care about them, it wouldn't matter what they said or did.

This is for you my friend.
The one person to take me just the way I am.
To accept with no changes
Wanting and taking me in, as a friend.

Your heart always so kind and loving,
When I see the sunrise I think of you.
Little by little making the earth warm,
Like your sweet smile.

Lighting the darkness of the night,
Helping me open my eyes,
To what has been done, to what has been said.
Realizing it's past,
Like the fair-weather friends.

You stayed with me when I was down,
And now I truly understand who was really the friend.

(16 years old)

A friend is someone who cares so deeply about you that they are able to sacrifice their own ideas or opinions for the moment in order to allow us to be ourselves. There is a willingness to accept our need for freedom to be who we are.

For myself, for as long as I can remember, I could count my real friends on one hand. Oh, we all have hundreds and hundreds of acquaintances, but a true friend is someone for whom I am willing to sacrifice. There is a loyalty involved, a commitment. When the times get rough, just see who has the strength or enough love to stick around and get burned in the process.

Friends can be considered family. You do whatever it takes, whatever the situation. Friendship is something that takes years to grow. And in a way, friendship is something which does have to be proven and earned. When you are considered a "best friend" you can be sure you are a very special human being.

During adolescence we may feel everyone has to be our friend. This is not so. It takes a lot of time, a lot of concern, and a lot of love. It is not something to take lightly, it is a feeling to be cherished for a lifetime. Even though . . . the circumstances may separate us along the way.

FRIENDS WHO MOVE ON . . .

My day seemed a little bleaker
*   again.*
It seems you have left me
*   to find a better friend.*

I am at a loss with unspoken words.
All I can manage to do
*   is remember.*

Where would a person be
*   without a memory?*
A memory is an entire life.
One seems to laugh
*   at the hard times*
because they are placed so neatly in the past.

Please.
Let there be no confusion.
"Something for conversation."
Just be yourself and I will be me.
Together
we shall find our friendship hidden and free.

My day seemed a little bleaker
*   again.*
My heart had a leak.
And my love seemed to be draining.

As a favor to me,
for old times sake,
please be my friend,
again.

(16 years old)

Obviously, I wrote this thinking a friend had deserted me. Sometimes we feel very possessive toward our friends. We want them to only be with us. We feel jealous when they start talking to other people. And if they decide they like that other person more, we feel really hurt.

It can be like finding a wild, injured animal; we care for it, help make it stronger, and then we have to let it go. It must have its freedom. It's the same thing for friends. Only if the freedom is allowed—will the friendship be true.

FRIENDS OF THE OPPOSITE SEX

You gave me bright city lights
full of dancing
Oh! So full of life
Long winding roads traveling
through a still night,
with drifting thoughts
beyond my sight.
Warm sunshine to soothe my soul,
And everlasting wisdom I will always know.

You gave me a hot desert sand,
falling stars   a glowing moon
lighting a mountainous land.
New faces.
Exotic places.

Time is irrelevant
it is a matter
of where it is chosen to be spent.

My friend,
You showed me how.
You taught me so well.
When, where and why.
Life; grasp it!
For it is nigh.

You never promised me tomorrow,
but you gave me your today.
You gave me a smile, a touch
And a dream
to send me on my way.

(19 years old)

Nearing adulthood something wonderful occurs. We begin to build friendships with the opposite sex. It may start out as a sexual attraction, but we are able to put the temptation aside. We realize the VALUE of friendship, and we allow it to grow. We may even decide to keep it on that level permanently, as true friends do not come along very often.

This is one of the most interesting and satisfying forms of friendships available to us as human beings. It helps us better understand the opposite sex, and can, in a way, better prepare us for marriage.

These friendships help us know the interests, thoughts, feelings, and motives (if I may be so bold) of persons of the opposite sex. As parents, we must realize the importance of these friendships. Adolescents must realize the importance of these friendships. They will help us throughout our lives.

We could devote an entire chapter or book on the value of friendships, but time and space make it impossible. We must explore other things. To close this section on frienship, I would like to share a poem one of my friends wrote. What it gives us is a look into the future, a maturing concept of the love that comes to us while we are still adolescents and our senses are at their peak, but have grown in a different direction. During our young adulthood.

MY SPECIAL FRIEND
by Mary Kay Hovanec

Thank you for being my friend
for being you,
relating to you
with you,
is fragile yet
be cautious, be sen-
sitive
take time please for indeed I like who I am
learning to know, to care about
to share with
I am close to.

Seeing you brings me much joy,
gives me a feeling of warmth,
of smiles and
laughter,
Perhaps of love
(not much at first)
but it's growing.

This is a difficult
relationship yours
and
mine but it is good;
  see I
need you now   this time   in my life
Come take my hand   walk
with me over the bridge
through troubled waters . . . needing each other no
longer
  then leave if you
  must . . .

But . . .   remember me   please,
  you cared
    you shared
  you loved,
    you brought
  me forth just
being yourself,

        Thank you
my friend.[1]

[1]*Sun Smile Thoughts,* by Mary Kay; Copyright 1976; Library of Congress. Permission granted by author.

CHAPTER THREE

Tears Often Shed
Void of Understanding

*P*ARENTAL INFLUENCE AND its effect will have a dramatic bearing on all of our actions during adolescence. Its effect may either be harmful or good . . . probably both. To say our relationships will be difficult during the adolescent years, is an understatement. Nothing will seem to make sense.

I think perhaps parents' drive for their kids' perfection lessens during these years. The excitement to stimulate learning ability, the strength to endure misunderstandings, and our appreciation of the youthful spirit, all diminish. And I believe, this drive in stimulating our children begins to diminish by the age of two.

While our children were infants we truly delighted in their every wave or unique motion. When they uttered their first word we listened in awe. Then something wonderful began to happen . . . communication.

Why does this begin to lose it's impact? Where do we lose it? The answer to "why" is probably because it's hard work to raise a child. We get tired day after day, year after year. It never ends. We can't wait until we can get them into nursery school or kindergarten. We can't wait until they're old enough for after school activities. And it's such a treat when they're playing at someone else's house.

Where do we lose it? It's probably in some invisible lost and found. A lost and found we will never be able to find. Because once those years are lost, we can never find them again.

While our children were infants, they depended on us in every area of survival. We were entranced with the concept that here before us lies a tiny, unique little being. One who loved us and cared for us no matter who or what we were.

As the child nears the age of two, however, we begin to realize just how unique this individual is. It frightens us. And that is when we begin to question if we will be strong enough to pull them through, to pull ourselves through, until they become adults. You think of all the hard work you're putting in, of all the love you're giving them. You wonder if it will all be worth it. And what will make it worth it? The answer lies in parental satisfaction. You must rely on your own satisfaction and nothing else. The satisfaction that you gave and you loved as hard as you COULD! You must not expect anything else in return. This is where we can go wrong. It is a job we don't get paid for and we do it because we WANT to.

I wonder . . . I really do. Am I giving all I can? Will MY daughter turn out to be a really neat person IF I have given all I can? I can't know. I will just have to wait and see. I will have to run on my own satisfaction, that I tried as hard as I could.

Boy, it IS hard work, isn't it? This hard work begins to gnaw at us. We feel like we need a break from all of it. It would be nice, wouldn't it? To take a vacation? Unfortunately, there are a lot of us taking our vacations during our children's adolescent years.

Let me give you an example of what can happen when we take a "vacation." We brought Jessica home from the hospital weighing four pounds. At home, she kept forgetting to breath. We had to shake her, tickle her foot, to remind her to take a breath. Was it nerve-racking? We took shifts. Every two hours we set the alarm and relieved each other. (I have to put this in right here because I couldn't believe it. I met a ninety year old woman who was two pounds when she was born. Her parents put her in a shoe box at the foot of their bed. Their feet kept her warm—like an incubator. They fed her with an eye dropper and kept her near their wood stove. Is life amazing . . . or what? At 90 she had more energy than I had at 30. I'm sure they took a vacation. My deal was a vacation compared to theirs. Okay, sorry, on with the story.) My husband and I spent every waking moment providing Jessica with positive stimulation with the hope she could catch up. During that first year I was laid up in bed for three days. Three days didn't seem long to me, but apparently it had to Jessica. She regressed in her progress three weeks.

Another quick example. Some friends took a two week trip and left their eight-month-old baby with Grandma. Grandma certainly loved the child, but what happened was the child became lethargic. She wouldn't eat. She slept and wouldn't get out of her crib until the parents returned. She had nothing medically wrong with her—she wanted Mom and Dad.

There is no way we can say we do not have a powerful impact on our children. We do. This impact continues throughout the adolescent years. We cannot take a break. We cannot take a vacation. We cannot relax and stop stimulating or motivating our children. For it is when we relax, kick off our shoes and let them run their lives by themselves . . . that is when the trouble begins.

RELATIONSHIPS

Our relationships with our parents are very special, but they can also be very difficult to understand. During a Bible study I belonged to, a question was raised: "Who do you think was the warmth in your youth?"

Surprisingly, the answers did not turn out to be our parents. Out of eight women, two said their mothers. Others mentioned various family members, mainly grandmothers and grandfathers. The others came up with aunts and uncles. What was so interesting was that the two women who mentioned their mothers, shared a similar background.

Both of these women said their mothers were not close to their OWN mothers. Both grandmothers had been involved in careers. They didn't view the family as a priority. So, when these children grew up and had children of their own they exerted an extra effort. They initiated a closer bond with their children. Obviously, it made an impact.

Actually, I was rather taken aback. I would have thought it would have gone the opposite, because the experts tell us we raise our children according to how we were raised. And . . . in thinking of all the child abuse in the world . . . it was nice to learn if we do exert an extra effort it can pay off.

The next question was: "Why didn't you feel especially close to your parents?"

"They didn't have the time for us. Working was more important than family. My mom and dad were always too tired."

Our motto, therefore, became "Stop and smell the roses." The housework can wait. The lawn can grow a little longer. Meals don't have to be fancy for company. Our children are going to be happy in spite of us!

I know. I know how difficult it is. I'm on a crash course right now to finish this book. I know my family is suffering. I would be stupid if I didn't. But it's short-term, and that is how I justify it. My husband must pick up the slack. And it's not like we didn't have to talk about it, or yell about it. It is very frustrating. I get up at three in the morning and work until seven. Then I work from one o'clock until four when my daughter's in kindergarten. I'll be damned if my own wants and needs take precedence over the ones I love. I have wanted to be a writer since I was eight years old. I have worked years and years to get this far, years of not being taken seriously... because one always writes for pleasure. Of course we do. It's not even pleasure, it's passion. It's like being in the medical field and seeing that body before you. The one that doesn't have a chance. It could have had a heart attack or it could be dying inside from loneliness. And somehow you touch it. It lives because somehow it has reached your warmth.

Do I expect my daughter to understand this? Sometimes I do. But I am wrong. And, I will have to put my typing away... because I have to stop and smell my little rose as she walks in the door from school. We will plop down in our big, comfy chair, hug and kiss and she will tell me what she has learned—or which boy tried to kiss her today.

MOTHERS AND DAUGHTERS
FATHERS AND SONS

Opposites go well together, and the family is no exception. Fathers and daughters get along better than mothers and daughters. Sons and mothers get along better than fathers and sons. And when the same sexes get together, let us just say, a little crisp friction may arise.

It is hard to understand, and one time I sat down and tried to figure it out. I was 21 and I wrote the following poem about this strange relationship.

FRIENDS FOREVER

Friends forever.
Finally understanding what has come to grow.
Having answers we at last choose to know.
Drifting blindly through years never ending,
Crawling, always falling,
In cryptic diversions along the way.

Tears often shed void of understanding.
Words which were spoken were;
Always confusing, sometimes abusing;
More than not, spitefully musing.

Pseudo meanings, sadistic answers, always avoiding;
TRUTH, which always chose distancy and annoyance.
Always measuring sorrowful ways
Of pain to be inflicted.

Prolonged, dismayed, disarrayed, and enraged!
Impassive, always impulsive, impertinent
Games played . . . but were never won.

Unanswered questions to life were left,
Uncertain smiles were always kept.
Unsympathizing TIME endowed;
Unembellished, nonreflected mercy.

We are silenced.
Immobilized.
Left with scattered, unsettled dust collecting at our feet.
Trying to climb the always present,
Never ending mountain which loomed majestically before us.
That crumbled beneath;
As we began to realize the threatening, nearing,
Forever ending . . .
Defeat.

Reaching higher.
Reaching longer.
Trying to survive.
Frantically hoping to stay noticeably ALIVE.

Earth stood deafly silent.
Living, giving, LIFE whispered . . .
Hush now . . . be quiet.

Grey distant sky disclosed,
Folded open, revealing;
Exhilarating, unforeseen, breathtaking;
LIGHT.
Unraveling heavens which had been to us . . . unknown.
Unblinded and struck by words of wisdom;
We silently knew we had unknowingly grown old.

TIME:
Had not stood quiet and misguided;
The beauty of loving spirit had been misplaced, forgotten;
It had been lost and left along the way.

Wisdom is given to those who wish to see;
That our friendship had always been;
And was forever meant to be.

Knotted bond between exists;
Binding understanding in open, giving hands;
Finally growing together at last!
There is love and caring to be had.
That which remained closed, now opened;
Like a flower prepared to bloom.

To feel . . . To touch . . . To understand . . . To treasure
Never forgetting to forever cherish.
A friendship blooming and growing with smiles;
With tender hands carefully grooming;
It shall forever last.

Giving . . . Caring . . . Learning . . . Sharing
Friends forever.
Never meant to be misplaced
Final understanding;
Open hands which are cast.

Friends forever.
It shall always be,
It shall forever last.

(21 years old)

Our relationships with our parents can be confusing, irrational, and loving at the same time. Perhaps it can be best said if we called it a "love-hate" relationship.

We want, but we don't want anyone to know. We need, but we don't want to admit it. We care, but we're afraid we care too much. We love, but what if they don't love us back?

We are stuck in a fog but can't find the way out. Our relationships with our parents should be one of the most important things in our lives. But are they? They are, but are they good? Sometimes we feel like killing each other. Both sides refuse to budge, they stand their ground that they're right—failing to even try and understand the other's point of view.

We need to be able to call "Time out." Look at it rationally, objectively. The child is seen as confused. But they have a right to be themselves. And, usually, the parent is always right, right?

Perhaps I started young with Jessica. Explaining the rationale behind everything. I just kept talking until I didn't know anymore—why something turns out or is the way it is. Sometimes there wasn't an answer, and we both accepted it. I would explain there was still a lot for us to learn. Now she is able to grasp the entire concept of something and is able to analyze it. And there are times, when she is right, and I am wrong. I will look at it objectively and find her reasoning sound. And I'll say, "You ARE right . . . good going!"

I think my favorite line in the poem is, "We are frantically hoping to stay noticeably alive." We are. We all are. But during adolescence it's at its height. We want to portray to the world that we do, indeed, exist.

During adolescence, there are times when everything is so negative around us that WE become negative. Sometimes during adolescence we may be experiencing so much negativism we may not even want to share the good in us. If we're perceived as being bad . . . we will be bad. If we're expected to flub it up . . . we will. All of us will. But we stick it to the adolescent even more.

RUNAWAYS

Our failure to comprehend, to understand and to love the adolescent may bring about a terrible dilemma. Our children may run away.

Empty faces.
Lonely faces,
Where will I be tonight?

Beneath the stars
and groping far,
For a new love
That can for once . . . be found.

Can it be bought?
Will it be fought?
Oh, lover!
Where can you be?
All I know is that you are far from me.

Fill this empty void.
There is a space in my heart,
One that can only be filled
By someone's tender touch.
Touch me!
All I ask is for a moment in your life.

Oh, these empty faces!
And these lonely places!
Can you find me in the crowd?

(17 years old)

The following is information taken from "Kids on the Run,"[2] by the Christopher News Notes. I feel this information is very pertinent to our subject.

"Estimates of the current number of runaways range from 600,000 to two million. Many runaways are back home within a week. Of those who don't return, only a handful ever reach one of the 700 shelters set up for them across the country.

Technically, not all of them are runaways. Some are what youth workers call 'throwaways'. . . youngsters forced out of their homes by abusive parents or made to feel unwelcome for economic reasons.

Officials of the Health and Human Services Administration say that more than half of all runaways have been physically abused, and that most are not reported missing by their parents.

An extensive survey of 14,000 households conducted by the Opinion Research Council of Princeton, NJ, revealed these facts about runaways aged 10 to 17.

- About three percent of the households with children in that age bracket had a runaway child.
- Most runaways are between the ages of 15 and 17.
- Almost half (47 percent) of the runaways are girls.
- The children of white-collar workers are as prone to leave home as those of blue-collar workers."

WHY DO THEY RUN?

The reasons for leaving home are as varied as the youngsters themselves.

Said Roberta Browne of San Bruno, CA, after being reunited with her family:

"I wasn't really serious about leaving at all . . . it wasn't my parents either . . . I guess everyone sometimes feels like they just have to get away, and that's what I felt like."

For some, however, running away is an act of self-preservation even though it is fraught with danger. On a Christopher Closeup television program, William Treanor, founder of the National Youth Work Alliance and a former runaway himself, observed:

"In a number of cases, family life has deteriorated to such an extent that making the decision . . . to leave can in fact be a fairly healthy decision."

[2]"Kids on the Run," copyright 1982, July-July No. 263, published by Christopher News Notes, 12 E. 48th St., New York, NY 10017. Reprint permission granted.

Says William L. Pierce, president of the National Committee for Adoption:

> "Sexual activity is one of the major reasons why young people run. In a few cases there is sexual abuse in the home. Or it may be a young man who has fathered a child out of wedlock and is concerned about his situation. Mostly, it's pregnant young women caught in a situation where she feels she can't stay at home, can't talk to anyone."

A study undertaken in Boston uncovered these reasons for leaving home:

> "I have no one to talk to at night." "My family did not want me." "It's better to get beat up by a stranger on the street than by someone you care about at home."

Still others cite reasons such as these:

> "My teachers picked on me." "I got in with a bad crowd." "I was always getting in trouble."

AFTER RUNNING WHAT?

Sometimes the experience of running away brings a change of heart.

Wendell Marthers ran away from his Pennsylvania home to find "movie stars, glamour and beach boys." Instead, he recalls being "scared just about every day."

And he was beaten up . . . six times. He returned home five years after leaving, having experienced the love of a California family that befriended him. Now he confesses:

> "It's kind of a shame when a person has to leave home . . . to learn he appreciates his own family."

However, one large runaway shelter reports that only 10 to 12 percent of the youngsters it serves are successfully reunited with their families. The others?

Some of them "develop families on the street," according to Lois Lee, director of Children of the Night, a Los Angeles program to help youngsters break away from prostitution. "They'll form groups and look out for each other."

Still, life is a struggle. Interviewed in St. Louis after three years on the streets of cities in the Midwest, Jerry Ulrich said:

> "At first you think you can take on the world when you're out on the street, but after a while it really gets tiring. There's a difference be-

tween surviving and living, and I'd give anything to be able to live right now instead of just surviving."

To survive, some youngsters turn to prostitution and crime. As Treanor observed:

"It is a very tiny minority . . . less than one-half of one per cent, if that . . . who are able to run away from home, to find a place to live, to find a job, and to establish themselves independently."

A few reach a runaway house. Dr. James Gordon of the National Institute of Mental Health says such temporary refuges offer young people "a time and a place for themselves, a chance to take a critical and often compassionate look at the families with which they have been hopelessly struggling . . . the family discovers that impasses may be broken, that choices are possible and that differences do not necessarily spell disaster."[2]

TEENAGE PROSTITUTION

Of the 730,000 to 1.25 million kids who run away each year—600,000 will become prostitutes. Many of us will believe they became prostitutes because they wanted to, when in all actuality they became victims of highly organized crime.

Children do not plan in advance to run away. They do not have a big bank account which allows them the luxury of a warm hotel room. They sleep or walk in the streets and are highly visible and vulnerable to the people looking for them. The people looking for them are either pimps, catchers, or recruiters. These people get paid $50–100 for each child—it doesn't matter what their age or what their sex. There is a market, and a lot of money is to be made.

The child will be brainwashed—stripped of any self-esteem. They will be beaten, threatened, blackmailed or held as slaves in a brothel. They will be forced to either sell drugs or their body in order to eat, and the money they make will be taken away.

These children will not know how to protect themselves and are constantly exposed to violence. It will not matter to the only person they trust, their pimp, if they die. The children are only one thing to him—and that is money.

The people the children will be forced to have sex with will range from 18 years old to 65. Ninety-five percent are white and married. Ironically, these customers will believe they are helping the child.

Many children run to the West Coast seeking glamour and fun. Los Angeles and the surrounding areas have over 300,000 children who are runaways. These children, however, may be transferred to another city or another country. Never to be seen again.

One of the organizations helping children on the West Coast is "Children of the Night," which is based in Los Angeles. It is a non-profit organization geared specifically to this problem.

RUNAWAY HOTLINE: 1-800-231-6946 or 1-800-621-4000

Children of the Night will help assess the situation, provide counseling, and can connect a runaway with the closest shelter, no matter where it is in the United States. If you would like more information on the organization Children of the Night, or if you would like to help, you can call or write: Lois Lee, Executive Director, Children of the Night, 1800 N. Highland, Suite 128, Hollywood, CA 90028, (213) 461-3160.

So working at a part-time job may not sound all that oppressive now. When I was in high school I had a friend. She was a really neat person, and we sat next to each other in class. She had a boyfriend she wanted me to meet. He was older than we were. I said, "Sure."

He picked us up from high school in a big car. It was the fanciest car I had ever seen. It was shiny, had all the extras, and it was a Cadillac. I didn't even know anyone with a Cadillac. I was impressed with this show of wealth. I thought my girlfriend was lucky to have such a rich boyfriend.

The two of them took me around to meet their other friends. They were all a different color, except the women. The women were white, and some of them were pregnant. I was impressed because their fingernails were long and brightly painted, and they got to watch soap operas all day long.

We also visited a big white house once full of women residents; there were about eight of them. Some of them were younger than I was, and they didn't have to go to school. They even got to dress like grownups; like grownups who go out to dinner.

I thought it was all very interesting, that it was a new way of life. I had nothing against inter-racial marriages, or children, really. They lived a different lifestyle, and that was okay.

Time went by, and the three of us had a good time. It was an interesting relationship between the two of them. I gave my friend credit for going against the grain, for taking a stand even though her parents disapproved. Her boyfriend had other friends, and I thought that was pretty neat—that you could have a boyfriend-girlfriend relationship and still keep members of the opposite sex as friends.

Only his friends of the opposite sex worked for him. Sometimes when we drove around we would go look for them. They would be standing outside fast food hamburger places. They dressed differently than I did. They wore high heels, short skirts, and black nylons. He would always ask how their day was going, and I thought that was real nice of him. They always answered, "Great!" Then they would hand him money.

I asked my girlfriend once what these women did for her boyfriend. She said, "You knoooow." I pretended I knew. But I didn't. I didn't know her boyfriend was a pimp.

My friend got pregnant, quit school, and moved into an apartment. Her boyfriend kept his own apartment, but they still saw each other. He was proud that he would soon become a father, again. I think he had three other children, all by different women. And the women were all friends. I started worrying about my friend.

I would visit her, and more than once she had a black eye. She would show me other bruises, on her arms, legs, chest, and back. A few times she told me about the sex they had had, and I couldn't understand it. But I was being cool, I listened, and pretended I understood. One of the things she said I'll never forget. She shouted to her boyfriend, "You keep her out of this!" It had been about me. I never saw my friend after that. I didn't know what it had meant, but I sensed it wasn't good. I'm glad I never went back. He had wanted me to be a prostitute.

There are many temptations in life. Usually it has to do with money. There are some of us who never learn. I am still learning. I still have to remind myself if something sounds too good to be true . . . it is.

I still like to think there's an easy answer to everything. An easy buck to be made if you're smart enough. Only, somehow, when the buck is made too easily, it's the smarter people who catch you. It's like, if YOU know it might be dishonest, there's a good chance some-one else out there thinks it's dishonest too.

The dishonest buck is everywhere, it's not only in prostitution. It's all over the adult world. We do it everyday when we stretch the potential or truth about a product or a business deal. It's in a lot of advertising when people sit down to pitch the best angle, to figure the best way to make people spend their money. It's in payola and special favors. It's in, "It's not what you know, but who you know." And you don't think our children hear us when we celebrate? "Boy, I didn't think I could do it. I didn't think they'd fall for it. But my presentation was SO good, I had all the angles covered, they couldn't come back with a single flaw, I really put one over on THEM . . . I sold three lemons today . . . you would have thought they would have at least ASKED, but am I going to tell them?"

Practically the first thing we learn in the world is how to manipulate to our advantage. Babies do it all the time. So what does this tell us, it's human nature? It probably is. To get the best result with the least amount of effort. With our children watching.

The moral of the story? Set a good example. You must teach your children money does not buy happiness. Money should never buy a body or your soul. Temptations will always be before us – but the price we initially pay is only the first installment.

Open those communication lines. Even if they have been closed for years. One has to start somewhere, and that is in the sharing of yourself. Time does not stand by, quiet and misguided . . . it marches on and on and on.

If you can't do it by yourself, seek professional help. These are people who have trained for years, and your problems will not be new to them. They specialize in problems. I know I cannot be objective all of the time. My friends and my family cannot be objective all of the time. Usually most of the time we can't be objective. We need to sort out our problems and put all of our ducks in a row. Life is very short, we have to keep track of it. We need to know we're moving forward and not backward.

MATURING DIFFERENCES

As we approach our adulthood, our relationship with our parents goes through a change. There is suddenly more understanding. It's about time, right? I think part of the reason is that now we look like adults. We look like we should know what we're doing. Besides, soon the parents will have an extra room in the house, and now . . . finally . . . it is time for that vacation. But WILL there be an empty room in the house? A lot of young adults are deciding to stay.

FAILURE TO LEAVE THE NEST?

There are a number of reasons why a young adult may choose to stay at home. The first possibility is financial. To leave home one must first have a job, and living expenses are always overwhelming no matter how old we are. What would the monthly cost to live alone be, or let's split it with one roommate. (Food, rent and telephone split.) Rent $250, heat $25, food $150–200, clothing $100, entertainment $100, transportation $75 (gas only), telephone $15. Seven hundred and sixty-five dollars for the essentials and that's not counting school. So easy to think about but very hard to manage.

If the adolescent is old enough to move out, they are no longer an adolescent . . . they are an adult. It may not seem like it to the parent, and I can understand this. However, wouldn't you rather have your child under your own roof, know they're eating right and still alive at the end of the day?

Rules must be drawn up like never before, and everyone must participate—every member of the household no matter what the age. It affects all of you. What are some of the things to be considered? Should rent be paid? (The minute I made a wage I paid rent.) Do household tasks change? Do responsibilities differ? What about curfews? Remember, if they were living on their own they wouldn't even have to come home at night.

A girlfriend of mine and her two children stayed with us for three months. Let's just say that any of us, at any time, can be down on our luck, and that is when family or friends need to hop in there and lend a helping hand. But let it also be said, that no, it was not easy. Besides personalities, schedules had to mesh. There were now three adults and three children to consider. Each child went to a different school, and two adults worked outside the home.

Every Sunday afternoon we organized our schedules for the coming week. Everybody got a copy of their responsibilities including which meals they would make, household chores, transportation of children to and from school, homework (who was good in math and who was good in reading), etc. Whatever crept up. The children were given a copy of the adult's schedule so they knew exactly where we were at all times.

All went pretty well until we discovered a little problem we hadn't considered. And actually, it was a problem that has come up with other single friends who were visting. My friend was divorced and had male friends. Of course I knew this before, but now it affected MY life.

People are always welcome in my home. An extra place can always be set at the dinner table. Extra beds, however, will never be made for sex. I will get into this more when we discuss single parenting, but you understand the correlation. You now have an extra adult in the house, even if it is your own child.

Sex is fine if you follow the rules (see chapter seven) and is between two consenting heterosexual adults. Remember, your child is now considered an adult. The young adult does have the right to invite friends into your house if they share responsibilities. They do not, however, have the *right* to have sex in your home. A clean hotel room for the night can cost as low as $20. Sex is between two people, not an entire family. Even a six-year-old can tell what's going on.

The crux of living at home as an adult is to sit down and think of anything that might create a problem, down to the smallest detail, so when it does crop up you can say, "Oh, yeah . . . we talked about that and we all decided this was what we were going to do . . ." Each side must discuss every issue with an open mind and compromise, even give in, if that's what it takes. You must come to a conclusion on each point and stick to it. But most of all, respect is the key. Respect in regard to each other's differences no matter what those differences may be.

TRADITION: A FAMILY AFFAIR

I wrote this five years ago: "I am truly frightened our society may be losing or has already lost touch with one of the most important aspects binding us together as a family. It has been sneaking away gradually, and we have not even noticed its demise or even considered reconciling its return to the century. The family tradition."

The dictionary defines tradition as "the passing down of elements of a culture from generation to generation, especially by oral communication."

We're too busy. We're too tired. And we're too commercial! We even celebrate birthdays on the wrong day if it isn't convenient for us. "We'll do it next week or two days from now." "We'll celebrate the two birthdays together."

If a child's birthday is on a Wednesday, we wait until Saturday for the party. And we wonder why our children suffer from a lack of self-esteem, when we fail to recognize the day they were born?

Birthdays are a big deal around here for us. That's because life is important. Usually we end up making three cakes for one birthday, and it's a week-long celebration. We gear up for the big day. We plan. Children always love to plan.

The day of the birthday we have a birthday dinner with just the family. We remind each other how important we are to each other. And we blow out the candles and scarf down the first cake. Then, nine times out of ten, Jessica will want to celebrate our birthdays with her neighborhood friends. They all think it's the neatest thing on this earth. Then we eat the second cake. Next, it gets to be Mom and Dad's turn. We go out to dinner or have friends over. And we eat the third cake. No, we do not weight 300 pounds. My husband weighs 220, but then he's 6'5" tall. Sure, it takes time. Sure, it's extra work. And sure, I go on a diet for a week. But life is so wonderful you have to SHARE it.

Structure, routine and tradition give us something to count on in life. We must think back about ten or twenty years in order to be able to relate to tradition. Tradition is simple, tradition is easy. It is sitting around a toasty fire with popcorn popping and a cup of hot chocolate to warm our insides on a cold winter's night. Singing songs around the piano while papa plays the violin off key. Taking turns reading a bedtime story even if we are too old to care. Beating Mom at Scrabble or Monopoly because everyone knows she doesn't know how to play anyway. Naming the states even if we are not sitting in a car. Talking. Going around the table . . . and talking.

> . . . . *Rebecca*
> *she teaches her arts to me.*
> *Over good conversation, deep secrets and tea.*
>
> *We needlepoint flowers and seagulls that fly,*
> *Sunsets and sailplanes as time passes by . . .*
>
> *(20 years old)*

Yes, we still do have a few traditions left in place. We sit around once a year to open presents, we fill our faces with turkey, and we hunt for eggs. This is not enough. We need more.

Our children need more. It doesn't matter to them if you're president of your company. It doesn't matter if you did or didn't get the raise. What matters is if you are THERE. In one study it said fathers spend an average of three minutes a day with their children. I suppose now there's a book called *The Three-Minute Father.*

Is this what we had in mind? Could we even fathom spending three minutes a day with our children while we felt them grow inside of us? When we heard their first cry for life? Our children are still crying for life. They cry for it every single day only we don't hear it. We are not listening.

A family is not a word you can look up in the dictionary. It is a feeling inside, a oneness with each other. It is a common bond, a thread that flows through each of us and forms a circle which protects us. It is loving, and it is touching one another. It is communicating our thoughts, our fears and our wants. It is laughing together. Enjoying life and each other. Wanting to spend the time.

It never ends. The things we want in life. Let us ask each other what we want out of life. We will say an object . . . not our children. We will say we want a new car . . . not a husband who loves us. We want a new dress, new carpeting, new wall paper, a cruise . . . not an impulsive hug from our children. We think we have happy homes, don't we? We will take it for granted it will always be there . . . like money grows on trees . . . so does love.

We measure our efforts only in terms of monetary value. If we work for three months we will be able to buy a new chair or a lamp. If we work three months on loving our children and improving communication within the family . . . it buys us . . . what?

Spending an hour with your child does not mean you still can't get things done. You talk and you hug each other while you both help fix dinner. You both wrestle with the towels while you're trying to fold them. You tickle each other and laugh. And whatever it is you're doing, will take twice or three times as long. Who cares? It gets done, doesn't it?

Make up a schedule if you have to, on the time you will spend together. Schedule a time every day you will be together, and schedule something special once a week. Don't allow any excuses or interruptions. And probably there will be some complaining, "Do I haaaave to?" Yes. You all have to. Before it's too late.

RELATIONSHIPS BETWEEN OUR FRIENDS' PARENTS AND US

Our relationships with our parents are very important, but another relationship to explore is one pertaining to our friends and their parents. Let me start out by saying that when we have other children in our house we have a responsibility. I don't care how old you are, your friends' parents represent a mother and father figure. They look to parents, whether they are their own or not, as something unique. We are expected to care for them, listen to them, and to love them. This is what children hope for. This is not necessarily what they find.

"They're not good enough for you."

Good enough for what? To take care of your dog while you're on vacation? To marry? To be a friend?

The really stupid thing of it is . . . we can positively influence our children's friends. It's up to us, if we want to take the time. That is, if we're taking enough time with our own children. They are ready to love you if you let them.

All you have to do is to be open to it. If your child has a friend, there is a reason they have chosen that friend. Don't you want to know why? Through our child's friends, we find out a lot about them . . . about ourselves. And usually, it's worth finding out.

It's interesting during adolescence. I had neighborhood friends and their parents always treated me like one of the family. That's probably because they knew me. They would have known if I was a drug addict. And I had friends located out of my neighborhood. I would imagine it's exactly like a boy meeting the parents on a first date. They look you up and down and size you up. They are afraid of you. You sense this anxiety but you don't know why. Their eyes don't see you, they see danger. They place every single danger they fear, on you. It's a pretty heavy load. But they don't talk to you, they just look at you. It might make you nervous. Oh, really?

What if parents were actually "friendly" to their child's friends? What if they accepted them as fellow human beings? A child is always quicker than we are. They see in a second what it takes us years to see. They see it in our eyes.

Children never really do understand "family trouble." They have a friend whom they love very much, and the parents come with the deal. The child is open, the child is willing, but then the door is slammed in his face.

I had a best friend when I was an adolescent. I called her up on the phone one night. She said she couldn't talk to me and then her mother came on the phone (the other line) and started screaming at me. She called me a slut.

I began to try to ask her why she thought this, but her reasoning was totally bizarre. I didn't even know what a slut was, but it sure didn't sound that great. I told her goodbye and hung up the phone. Then I started crying. My parents asked me what was wrong, and I was afraid to tell them. What if they believed whatever the word meant? Well, they didn't, and they drove over to her house to straighten it out.

My parents are nonviolent people, they talk things out. My friend's parents weren't ones to talk things out, they shouted them out and probably threw a fist or two. My parents returned shaking their heads in disbelief. They mentioned family problems. They advised me to stay away from my friend, to see her at school but to stay away from the house.

Yes, it affected me. I looked the word up in the dictionary and felt like scum for about two weeks. I would have liked to have been friends with her parents. And there had been many things going on in my friend's life besides my friendship with her. But you have to put the blame on someone when your children aren't doing what you think they should be doing, don't you? It can't possibly be the child's problem or the parent's, right?

About two weeks later something completely opposite happened. I had another friend whom I referred to as the "slave." She was allowed an hour every week to see a friend. You see, they ran a VERY tight ship in their house. Every time I called her she was doing something like washing walls, varnishing woodwork, canning peaches, washing every can in the cupboard . . . things that all 16-year-olds should be doing. She was given 15 minutes a day to sit by herself, and it was timed.

Her parents hated every single one of her friends. Yes, it was a good situation to walk into. I can remember driving in the car with my friend and her father. He wanted to know what my plans for life were, what I would be doing when I was 30. He wanted to know what I thought about all the teen-agers these days. Then he wanted to know my views on movies, all the violence and sex they portrayed. I told him my favorite movies were Walt Disney movies. I think I mentioned the ones with Fred McMurray. He liked me. I thought it made a lot of sense. I was the only one she was allowed to play with after that.

SINGLE PARENTING

One cannot possibly fit what should be said on single parenting in one little section, this is a biggie and would require an entire volume. We can, however, touch on a few of the problems.

Whether you are male or female and have custody of your child or children, it is imperative they have a role model for each sex. Role models do not usually come in the form of sexual partners, but in friends. You need to have a friend of the opposite sex who can be a role model for your child. And pick your friend wisely.

I'll give you a quick example on how strong this need is. It happened just last night. My daughter had a little friend stay overnight. We had dinner together, sat around after dinner together, and I gave them baths. After spending four hours in our home and being involved with a family where everyone participates . . . she wanted to call my husband Daddy. It's the next day right now, and the three of them are out for a walk.

Her mother was divorced and now she's going through another divorce. My daughter's friend says things like, "Boy, my dads don't ever talk to me, you're really lucky. My dads don't ever do things that I want to do, you're really lucky." It makes me want to cry. It's all so simple if you just take the time.

Taking your kids to a movie when you have them on the weekend is very convenient. You don't have to talk to them. You sit in the dark and you don't even have to look at them. Sure, you can take them to a basketball game, but you don't have to talk to them there, either. Take a walk with them. Choose an activity in which you can converse. Of course you're going to find out your kids are hurting. But they know you're hurting too. It's not an easy situation, but you CAN make it better.

It is usually the mother who has custody nowadays. And life is not easy. The father may have the children on the weekends, but the mom tries to be mom *and* dad the other five days. Again, just as with tradition, you must schedule time every day. You must schedule something special once a week. If you have more than one child, spend specific time with each one, then spend time with both of them. They must know even if the family has been separated, there is no separation between the two of you.

The single mother is going to be very busy. No doubt, she works outside the home. Her time is very valuable, and she must be organized like never before. Sit down on Sunday and make out a schedule for the week. This will also help the children. They will know there is still routine and consistency left in their lives.

Monday through Friday: You get home at six o'clock every evening. You children are waiting for you. You have them do their homework as soon as they get home from school. You schedule evening meals, and the kids start the dinner every night. You eat dinner at six-thirty. From seven-fifteen to quarter to eight you clean the kitchen. At eight o'clock you do not sit down to watch television. You spend an hour with either all of your children or just one doing something constructive or just plain talking. (That's constructive.) At nine o'clock you take baths, and each one of you takes care of what they have to. From nine-thirty to ten you all sit down and relax together, either watching TV or reading. But you do it in the same room . . . together.

You pick one day out of the week when you all have an activity. It must be on the same evening. That gives you four evenings a week to bond. Weekends are somewhat free—in a sense. This is when you get your laundry and housework done. All the kids pitch in from ten to two on Saturday. From two until four or five, Mom does the shopping. She picks up ingredients for six meals. Then everybody has a free Saturday night. Sundays are open, but come four or five o'clock, you all sit down together and work out next week's schedule, eat dinner and relax.

No, it's not going to be easy, but then nobody ever said it would be. The single parent must work double compared to a two parent family. It can be done, you can keep your family intact. Give the schedule a try. There may be moans about it, but at least give it a try. What will probably happen is that you'll all get used to it, and it will become the norm in your life. Life gets too scattered when you're single with children. It is imperative you have routine, consistency, and a whole lot of love to go around.

SEX AND THE SINGLE PARENT

During adolescence the child will have very confusing views on sex, himself, and how to relate to both. Television tells us a lot of things, but your actions will say more. We all have sexual urges beginning from birth, and these urges do need to be fulfilled. It makes us healthy human beings. To put it rather bluntly, however, let's not fulfill them in front of the children.

Children are not naive. They know what is taking place. It does not help to sneak the friend in after they are asleep only to have them disappear by morning. They can hear your voices or the bathroom door closing five or six times, even in their sleep. They know.

And don't forget, hotels can be cheap. That doesn't have to mean you are. Personally, I'd rather have a stranger at the desk wondering about me than my own child. And if your partner doesn't want to shell out for privacy . . . it's not worth it. You are worth a lot more.

If you are serious about someone, very serious, sit down with your child and discuss it. They have a right to have a say in the matter, because it does affect them. Whether you know it or not. If you are not serious . . . don't let them know, for it is better not knowing in some instances. There are ways and places where urges can be fulfilled other than within a house full of adolescents or children. Let us keep what should be private in the first place . . . private in the last place.

ROLE MODELS

There comes a time in every adolescent's life when a special respect for an older adult occurs. They look up to them, they may mimic their actions or style, they become aware that they want to be like this person. They have discovered a role model.

The quality we are attracted to is a simple one. They believe in us. They see qualities worthy of time, energy and respect. It's like turning around and saying, "Who me? Is something wrong?"

"Do I have a zipper undone or something?"

"A piece of toilet paper on my shoe?"

No, it is the beauty within us they see. It gives us a glimpse into our futures, and we feel like we can really make it in the world after all. When people other than our family and friends believe in us, it helps us to believe in ourselves.

Adult role models can be either good or bad. I had an experience once with a bad role model. It was with a typing teacher in high school.

I looked up to him, as we look up to most adults during that age. He gave us a typing assignment to do at home. He wanted us to type out our own stories. I had never written a story before, and I threw myself into the project. But I only had ten pages done. It was about a girl riding in her car down a country road. She was feeling a little blue, and then she came to a meadow with a horse. She loved horses, and they formed a friendship.

We turned our assignments in, and he shuffled through the papers. I could see him shaking his head as he sat behind his desk. He got up from behind it and approached the class. He said, "I'm only going to read one story out loud. The rest of you did a really fine job." He began reading my story out loud, and I looked around to watch the other people. I felt so proud. He began reading it the way it was supposed to have been read, and then his voice changed. He was reading it faster, like it didn't matter what the words meant. It didn't matter what my character thought. He didn't finish what I had written. "This," he said shaking the paper at me, "is a classic form of plagiarism. Do you know what plagiarism is, class? It's when you take words that someone else has written and you tell people YOU wrote them."

My face was getting redder every second. I didn't know if I could even speak. I barely got the words out, "I wrote that."

"Excuse me?" he replied very nastily.

"I said . . . I wrote that."

"If you want to go on and believe that, it's up to you," he said shaking his head.

"I really DID write it," I insisted.

He didn't comment, and went on with the class. I wanted to run out of the room, and his attention towards me after that was minimal.

I never attempted to write a story until I was 25. Even though deep down I knew he must have thought my story was good to have done that to me, it had killed something inside of me. It made me afraid to try again.

How can teachers do this to us? I don't know, but they do, and it really only takes a second. They can kill a dream of a lifetime. And once again, it is important that communication lines are open between parent and child. The parent must be there to explain the situation objectively, do what is right, and follow through.

I had a very good experience another time. It was with an English teacher I had for study hall. I had been writing many of the poems that are in this book, and I showed them to her. She thought they were wonderful. Well, I thought, if I can't write a story I'll at least write a poem.

We sat down together and she took the time to go through each one. We talked about them, what they meant and on and on. She gave me a certain hope inside. That maybe there was something there.

I have never forgotten her. I'll remember her forever. I sent her a copy of the first story I had published. I never heard back from her, but that's okay. She didn't need to send me a letter, she had already given me something important. Belief in myself.

PARENT ROLE MODELS

Which brings us to parent role models. Mothers work today. And fathers work. This does not mean we still can't be "Mom" and "Dad." Everybody talks about "quality time"—that it doesn't matter how much time you spend with your children as long as it's quality time. If that's ALL you can give, then it will have to do . . . but WE are the most important role models of all.

I provided my child with quality time for about a year. I was offered a job with a corporation for a lot of money. I had been at home struggling with words on paper, and then a miracle happened. Someone wanted to pay me for writing words. And actually, do the same things I do at home, but differently—on a grander scale so to speak. Instead of organizing birthday parties, dinners and repairmen, I organized store openings and employees.

People actually took me seriously. Adults wanted to know what I thought, and applauded me for it. I was like a kid in a candy store. I even got to dress up and look nice. And I buzzed here and I buzzed there, in town and out of town, while my child sat in a daycare.

I had read all about putting children in daycares and about mothers working. It was okay. Children broadened their horizons. And Jessica still knew I loved her. She had to. Because I gave her quality time.

Every time she said, "But . . ." in the morning, I had a reason for her. I convinced her she was doing well where she was. And at the dinner table every evening when she said, "But . . ." I nodded to her and told her how exciting it would be for her to see her mother on television commercials.

I could mix socially and sometimes be smarter than the men. I talked their jargon. They asked me my opinion on things. They respected me. It was a different respect than what you get from a household of kids. You really have to WORK for THEIR respect. I always laughed to myself and said, "I can't believe how easy this is . . . and I'm making money!"

It was a breeze. If you run a tight ship at home and do it well . . . you can do it in business. I ran rings around them. When salesmen entered my office I almost asked them to wipe their feet or take off their shoes. In negotiating, I couldn't be beat. I beat them. Instead of negotiating on which child gets what toy or what kid said what to whom, I was working with thousands of dollars. Hundreds of thousands of dollars. I could now measure my worth as a human being.

Jessica could now measure my worth also, because I bought her more toys. I took her on vacation with me to Florida. She could go swimming and collect seashells. Except, I was too tired to go with her. I was on vacation. But I'm sure she enjoyed herself as I sat and talked with two girlfriends about which angles were best in getting what you wanted in the business world, sexual harassment, and employee relations.

The other shoe dropped when I returned to work. They didn't need me anymore. I had systemized myself out of a job. I couldn't accept someone not needing me . . . I was always needed before. I couldn't turn around without someone needing me to do something in my HOUSE. I went through months of sulking and feeling sorry for myself. I didn't want to run the house. It was beneath me. There were more important things I could do, and do them well. I didn't want to write . . . I couldn't write. I couldn't cook a roast. I didn't want to. I wanted my own advertising firm. I wanted to feel the beat of the corporate world, the pulse of life. I went through "corporate withdrawl."

Each day my child came up to me and asked if I could help her with something. I painstakingly said, "Yes." So I sat and colored with her. There was nothing else to do. I would have rather been writing radio and television commercials. She'd put her arms around me and say, "I'm glad you're home." I wasn't. I'd try to smile and then say, "Yes, it is special, isn't it?" out of the corner of my mouth.

I got used to the coloring and playing Barbies. We made up elaborate plots and sets. I taught her how to cook. We talked about things that were important to her for hours on end. We went on "adventures" discovering something new every day. I began to try to teach her everything I could. It spurred on a new curiosity. Our coloring turned into designing. At ten o'clock at night she was making paper airplanes and she wanted to know all about them. She knew planes flew but wanted to know why. I explained engines, lift, drag and ailerons as best I could. She understood. Then finally a light bulb went off in my head. I went back to my husband and said, "Do you realize what time it is?" He said, "Yes." I went on. "I can't believe we're sitting in the kitchen and I'm teaching Jessica about lift, drag and ailerons. She wants to know MORE. Do you know anymore?"

The potential is unlimited in what children can learn. The only way they will learn is if we take the time to teach them. Sometimes we are forced to take the time, and at other times we have to realize it ourselves.

I decided to stay at home and give writing another try. What happened was very interesting. I began to watch the children at play. It was evident playing house was very important to them. And the way they played changed. In the beginning they played traditional roles, like back in the olden days. The man of the house went to work and the mother stayed at home to cook and take care of the children. They both spent a lot of time with their children. Then, they both went to work and both of them cooked. There was an absence of children in their play and I asked them why. "We're both working, and we don't have time." They both traveled a lot too to Hawaii and Kansas City.

After months, it changed again. They both worked, but it was for shorter amounts of time. They had children this time. Only they always brought their children with them, they incorporated them into their lives whether it was at work, at home, or going on trips. They put their children in their briefcases.

To say I'm glad to be at home is rather unimportant now. I could have gone out and gotten a job at any time along the way. But I realize my worth as never before. In the beginning of kindergarten Jessica was learning letters and sounds. She was doing quite well, but I knew she was capable of better. I hadn't realized children have to learn how to "read" letters and numbers. I asked for guidelines from her teacher on what they were supposed to learn. Sure, she would have learned eventually, and she would have done alright. We spent a total of four hours one week in two areas. She learned what would have taken a year to learn in school on those two specifics.

I was talking to my husband a few months ago, and said, "Can you believe how far she's come? Just because I'm here everyday? It's a full-time job around here. I don't know how I did it when I was 'working." Well, I didn't do it while I was working. Life was hectic and we were only existing. We weren't "living."

I looked back at the year and a half I had worked outside the home. I had worked to make money and fulfill my needs. My need to feel important. I remembered back to when I was single and had worked in an emergency room. I was driving home one day looking at the trees. I couldn't see the beauty in that single tree any longer. I knew something was wrong. I didn't want to ever lose that feeling, but I had. I wondered if I could get it back. I changed occupations and it took awhile, but it did come back.

It had been the same when I worked in the corporate world. After

I was let go I cried for a month. I hadn't looked at a tree. I had been too busy. I looked out the window to see the trees. I had lost it again. I couldn't see the beauty. It took about four months to get it back, with the help of my little one showing me the way. For it wasn't just the beauty of a tree I was looking for . . . it was the beauty of life.

Learning how to become and stay a parent takes a lot of work. Our children learn how to become parents from us. We must teach them. They are like sponges when it comes to learning. I know many women are forced to work. But we must organize ourselves better. We spend so much time justifying our guilt, rationalizing why we shouldn't be at home. That's because we know inside we are just as good as any man out there in the business world. Darn right we are! We can even do it better. But why do we have to try to prove it so hard and get spit on in the process? It is harder to stay at home than it is to join the workplace. It needs to be a decision inside yourself which is more important. And even if you do decide to stay at home and be with your children, your husband will probably not thank you. Your children will not thank you. But if your child decides to stay away from drugs, doesn't try to kill herself and has a healthy attitude . . . isn't that thanks enough?

Ask your children the question, "Would you rather have me home?" They will say, "Yes . . . but I like the extra money." Then ask them which is more important. I already know the answer.

We don't have to sit home and pick lint off the carpet or count the hairballs on the dog. There is much to do. If we gave our families as much as we gave our employers, we'd all be running the most successful company in the world. The family. The family-business. It is a business, and it should be run like one. Instead of producing products, you'll be producing people. Some pretty neat people, at that. That's the pay-off. That's your reward. Work around your children, don't make them work around you. Give them the best role model in the world. You.

PARENTAL INFLUENCE SUMMARY

In trying as a parent to conjure up a message of what I would like my own daughter to know or to have, or in attempting to put my own views of parenthood into perspective, I wrote:

Dear Jessica:

You have put me in such a difficult position. Or do I realize I am the one who put myself within these thick walls of responsibility? Little did I realize the strength it would take to hold on to your tiny hand. The hand I have sometimes smothered and often cradled inside of mine.

I think back to the many times when my heart was shattered or feelings hurt because of some small word, glance or gesture taken. To say I would like to shelter you from these evils is unrealistic. It seems so unfair, so unreal for me to explain my purpose in life as to allow for disappointment to drift into your small, safe world a little at a time. And then hope this will make you strong for what lies ahead.

. . . the sharing of your favorite toy when all you understand are your own wants and needs. Saying, "No," to a sugar cookie because I want only good things to enter your body. The insistence on rest because you live and play with such a fierce abandonment, my child . . . my dear Jessica. I let you fall a short distance hoping you will understand a small hurt may prevent a larger one. I carefully place other people in your life with the hope you will be able to visualize what individuality is and means, how very important it is to cherish and nurture . . .

I see so much of myself in you it frightens me. I wish I were a magical genie and could place you exactly where I am at this point in my life . . . knowing full well how many hurdles and paths I have jumped and crossed just to get this far. But I realize I cannot do this, I am only your mother. So I worry and I dream and I hope your spirit will not be damaged through all that lies ahead.

I wish you lived in a fairyland where dragons were always slain by a handsome prince and you would never have to feel the heat of their fire. I wish learning came instantly never accompanied by pain and anguish . . . which is truly inevitable. I would do anything if I could bear the pain for you.

Yes, I know you are a survivor, and you fought so very hard for your life. This does make it a little easier knowing how strong you are, but not much. My stomach churns and my heart aches every time I see a flash of disappointment in your eyes. My heart jumps and hysterically leaps when I see a dash of excitement or a glimpse of love shining through . . . just knowing I had a part in your creation.

Sleep now my little baby. Mommy will chase those green dragons away when they come to steal any part of your perfection or innocence. I will be here to always give you hope, support and serenity when their fire gets too hot . . . I promise. Forever and ever. For my heart is a part of your heart, and I truly do feel the pain and joy when you feel it. I hope I always can. Sweet dreams my little one. I love you.

Times are rough out there, and the temptations are great. It is not going to get easier – it will get harder. The only solution in winning the battle of adolescence is within the family. There are too many things out there that can catch us without our even knowing it. The family has to stick together like glue and become a FORTRESS. It must become a SHELTER we can run to. Because if we don't have anywhere to run to . . . we're going to get run over.

WHO ELSE CAN HELP?

If communities would take the time, they can help adolescents. Our community has events going on every weekend for kids. And they usually have something going on during the week. You simply have to give kids something to do if the parent is not around. And, communities can tell their children they love them. In Eden Prairie, Minnesota, a suburb of Minneapolis/St. Paul, the mayor declared the month of February as "Eden Prairie Loves Its Kids" month. It goes like this, if you would like to adopt something similar:

RESOLUTION NO. 87-8
CITY OF EDEN PRAIRIE
RESOLUTION PROCLAIMING FEBRUARY, 1987,
AS "EDEN PRAIRIE LOVES ITS KIDS" MONTH

I, Mayor Gary Peterson, of the City of Eden Prairie, Minnesota, do hereby officially declare and proclaim the month of February, 1987, as "Eden Prairie Loves Its Kids" month. It is to commence on February 1st, and end February 28, 1987.

I hereby proclaim that:

The month of February, 1987, be dedicated to all of our kids in the City of Eden Prairie . . . from the newborn infants born, or kids adopted, this very day to Eden Prairie couples, the toddlers, preschoolers, nursery school kids, kindergarten kids, elementary kids, kids in junior high at Central Middle School, and the students at Eden Prairie High School.

I hereby proclaim and encourage every resident, every parent, every church, every school, every community club and organization, every employer and business establishment in Eden Prairie, to take an active part in "Eden Prairie Loves Its Kids" month.

I hereby encourage everyone in our City of Eden Prairie to join our hearts together in a 100% community effort and team support to show our kids how much they are loved and appreciated. Our goal will be an honest effort to try and raise self-esteem, and hopefully, we will be able to reach the kids in our City who have had far too many "hurts and struggles" in their young lives. Also, I proclaim that the kids who are achieving success be highly complimented, and be given special recognition for their accomplishments during the month of February.

I hereby encourage every citizen of Eden Prairie to report any suspicions of child abuse or neglect, the selling of alcoholic beverages to minors by any local liquor establishment, or the dealing of drugs in our City, or the selling of drugs by anyone to our kids, to please report your suspicions to the Eden Prairie Public Safety Department . . . They are always willing to check it out, and proceed from there with appropriate action, if necessary.

I hereby proclaim that no monetary rewards or gifts be given to our kids in conjunction with "Eden Prairie Loves Its Kids" month, other than the cost of sponsoring a meal or activity in appreciation of our kids. I proclaim that the gifts of love and feelings flow freely during this special month, such as hugs, smiles, pats on the back, or loving words of expression and encouragement, etc.

I hereby encourage everyone in Eden Prairie to become actively involved in a community-wide effort of all the people of our City. We may not be the only city in America dealing with struggling, hurting, and acting out kids, but let it be recognized that we the people of Eden Prairie, Minnesota, U.S.A. will be trying very hard to help some of our kids, instead of sitting back in shock and amazement, and that February, 1987, will become known in our City as "Eden Prairie Loves Its Kids" month, and hopefully, some of the ideas, etc. from February, will continue into the future years.

For further information on organizing activities for the month of February, please call Dottie Ewert at . . .

Adopted by the Eden Prairie City Council this 6th day of January, 1987.

The evidence of "Eden Prairie Loves Its Kids" month is indicated throughout the city. You walk into stores and there are banners letting the kids know we love them. Everybody has a smile on their face. If you walk into a shopping mall you will see pictures the little ones have drawn depicting what it all means.

The program was conceived by an Eden Prairie resident, Dottie Ewert, who is also a member of the Eden Prairie Toughlove parent support group. The final day of the program, a balloon launch was made from a local park. Tied to the balloons was a message which read: "This balloon was launched from Round Lake Park in Eden Prairie, Minnesota, February 28, 1987. A community effort to express our love for our children. If found, please send its location and this tag to: . . . Please write your wish for your child in the open space and sign your name."

The message of the program traveled across the state, and the group is receiving many tags and wishes from all over. Many local businesses helped with the project and donated services and products to be used. Your community could very easily adopt something similar to help raise your kids' self-esteem. All it takes is the effort and the time. Our kids are worth it.

If you would like information on Toughlove, you can write them at TOUGHLOVE, P.O. Box 1069, Doylestown, PA 18901, send a self-addressed, stamped #10 envelope, or call (215) 348-7090. Toughlove is a parent-support-group and there are over 2,000 Toughlove parent support groups throughout the United States and in four other nations.

We can also reach kids through the media. The Minneapolis Star and Tribune has something called Mindworks. They pose a question for the kids, the kids write in with their answers or thoughts, and at least one full page of the newspaper is dedicated to their "minds."

We could reach teenagers through television. I have a bit of a background in television, and came up with an idea one evening. It's actually quite simple, and anybody could do it.

It's basically a "For Kids, by Kids" talk show. Most cities have a cable access channel available to regular citizens. All we have to do is take advantage of it. It doesn't have to be fancy. Your set can be a few chairs and a telephone. An adult sits in as a host, and you get four or five kids to volunteer from the local high school. The object is for teens to call in on the telephone, they don't have to say their name, but they must give their age. Then they ask the panel of teenagers a question, or tell them about a situation that's troubling them. (Remember, no swearing or it won't work.) The panel takes turns speaking on how they would solve the problem or air their views. The adult host can give her point of view. Parents can also call in and ask the teens a question.

I would recommend taping be done on a Saturday morning, having it be a weekly talk show (for consistency), and airing it Sunday evening about six-thirty. And, as far as the cameras go, there are a lot of students in high school who know how to use them. The show could even be produced by students.

When I talked with a few kids about the show I was wary. I had forgotten how receptive they can be. They got so excited I couldn't believe it. They were astounded someone would want to know what they thought. They were even more astounded an adult would let them give the ANSWERS. I hope all of you decide to give it a try. The benefits would be many. The cost would be minimal. It would be educational for parents and teens.

Local businesses can help. They can start Business/Education Partnerships. A Business/Education Partnership is when a business gets together with a school for a common goal. The partnerships can come in many forms. I helped start an incentive program where we supplied small, inexpensive items to a grade school. (Nuts and bolts are great for teaching counting!) The teachers held a number of meetings to decide exactly how they would use the items. It is important a business lets the school and teachers decide how they would like to incorporate you into their school. Our teachers decided they would use the items as an incentive in the areas of reading, math and social studies. If the students read so many books they received a coupon. Each week the coupons were collected and put in a bin.

Then names were drawn and those students received a "prize" for their achievement. Reading skills improved throughout the school. At first, the teachers were a bit skeptical. We had to be careful, it had to be viewed by the students as meeting a goal. We incorporated both tangible and intangible rewards into the program.

An entire classroom can also work on goal setting. This is a great way for them to learn how groups can work together to meet a goal.

We had a program called "Catch A Student Being Good." Every employee in the school participated. Each employee was given tokens to hand to kids when they caught them being good such as, walking quietly in the halls, standing in line very still, not shouting, not pushing, etc. When the children accumulated so many tokens, they could "purchase" something at the school store such as a new pencil, erasers, etc. Walking through the halls was amazing, the most orderly school I've ever seen. When things are in order, you learn better.

Businesses also benefit from this partnership. It's a give and take situation. Our trade-off came in many ways. The children made cards and pictures, and we displayed them in our stores. It promoted good community relations. And, if you're creative enough about it, you can get free press. The media loves to hear about businesses and schools working together toward a common goal – better education. Teachers, themselves, have many things to offer. You would be amazed at how many problems they can solve in regard to business . . . if you ask them. You can also trade time, tours, and speakers.

Rewards come in many forms. It had been two years since I had worked on the program, and a parent called me. They had moved out of the school district, and she wanted to know how to start a Business/Education Partnership in their new school. She thought the program had really made a difference. It had helped our business too . . . it goes both ways.

CHAPTER FOUR

I Never Promised
You Tomorrow

*T*RAVELING THROUGH ADOLESCENCE we are faced with a new, unfamiliar disease. A disease that does not affect us as children for we have never had to encompass its lingering, aching pain. It is a disease that can eat a devastating hole or cause a gash right through our very souls. It has the ability to engulf us so completely, we feel nothing else. It will strike every single one of us at different times in our lives, and there is no known cure. It's name is loneliness.

The bench is now empty
awaiting its new customer
loneliness.
Somehow, loneliness
is always present.

Time has no ending.
Its dials
always pass over what is real.
Time turns into a bomb,
ready to explode
at a faint quake
of fear
love
anger or happiness.

But loneliness does not faze it.
Time goes on . . . in time.

There is now a lineup
awaiting the bench.
I am its first customer.

(16 years old)

75

LONELINESS

The purpose of devoting an entire chapter to loneliness is because it is one of the hardest, most difficult things to deal with during adolescence. It can be most difficult to cope with, understand and to endure. Our failure to cope with this feeling can bring on drug abuse, suicidal tendencies, or suicide itself. It can also bring on a child born to a teenager. Why loneliness does exist, is simple. We feel all alone.

Do you know the feeling to be alone?
Separated from the crowd,
Being the joke?
Being alone is lonely.

You long for someone
to run to
reach out and grasp!
Alone is to see beauty,
have a nightmare,
and have nobody to share it with.

No one to share,
to give yourself to,
exert effort
for a smile, a touch;
someone to love,
to love you.

I will love you
if you are alone and lonely.
Let me.
You might like it you know.
Pride has no place in love.

(16 years old)

During adolescence we become frightfully aware that in spite of belonging to a family unit or belonging to our peer group, we stand alone. There is a brutal realization we really only have one person to rely on throughout our lives . . . and that is ourselves.

We discover others whom we have counted on up to now, were or are not always right. It's like waking up one morning and becoming aware during a simple conversation, something irrelevant slips out of our parents' mouths. It is realizing their answer or comment sounds "dumb," and we know we have a better answer . . . at least for ourselves. We can become frantic, hoping there is someone out there who really does have an answer . . . and we are devastated when we realize nobody does.

A young girl sits
huddled in a corner.
She seems . . . lonely.

Look at the way her eyes
are like glass with her tears
appearing as windows.

I wonder what she sees,
could she see me?
A lonely person too?
Does she realize she is not alone
being lonely?

It's too bad the lonely
never find each other.
Each searching
for someone
to take the torment away.
Their tears blinding their sight.

I am here.
I will be lonely with you.
Or do you want to be alone?

(16 years old)

We find comfort in many ways. But loneliness finds us when we least expect it, and it does not disappear instantly. It can stay with us for a very long time. Loneliness is different for the adolescent. We don't find solace in simply keeping busy, and we can feel lonely in the midst of a crowd. Unfortunately at this age, we don't know our best friend is not even two inches away at all times. Our best friend is inside of us. Our best friend is us.

UNHEALTHY SOLUTIONS

I believe our first awareness of what loneliness really is surfaces around the ages of 11 and 12. At these ages, however, we are able to brush this feeling away, basically, because it brings us a pain we know we do not like. But, by the ages of 15 and 16, we discover we are

unable to dismiss this ache knocking at our hearts, and we may look
to an alternative that is quickly available in order to dull the pain.

The flickering candlelight
brings my mind so wide awake.
The incense floats around
making me high on its smoke.

The night so calm . . . so peaceful
I hardly know what to expect from its beauty.
So peaceful . . . calming my soul
making me shut out all the hassles
the shrieking laughter
that makes no sense at all.

I wish I could share this beautiful feeling
if someone would stop and take a glance
I would share myself,
do you give a damn?

I guess I cannot make you stay.
It is your choice to stay or go.
But please . . .
if it is me you are laughing at,
go.

(15 years old)

Obviously, you know how I felt while writing this, but where I was,
was rather unusual. I was 15 and on a church retreat. Of course, our
parents were thrilled we were doing something so wonderful . . . getting back to nature, touching base with God. And we were safe, nothing could harm us.

Oh, yes, we had fun. Everybody had a lot of fun making-out, staying up all night, and getting stoned. Marijuana was fairly new at
that time. Those were the hippie days, Woodstock, and all that. We
didn't know it would harm us, give us cancer, or that it was illegal.
Well, we knew it was illegal, but we didn't care. And nobody knew,
the chaperones never knew, what was going on. And I felt all alone
because I wasn't doing it.

Here we all were, gathered together to be united as one, and we
weren't. At least I felt no connection whatsoever. The Vietnam War
was in the beginning stages, and I couldn't understand why everybody else did not comprehend what was happening. It seemed as

though they could not care less. Who knows? Maybe they did care, maybe they were trying not to think about it by getting stoned.

My feelings fluctuated between seeing all the beauty of the world, but of also seeing all the pain and anguish accompanying it. I felt alone because apparently no one was comprehending at the same level I was. "So what can we do about all the pain, anguish, and war? That's our parents' problem."

I was, however, realizing only too well it was becoming our problem. Many of the boys making-out would soon be shooting automatic rifles and machine guns. Some of them would die.

They giggled and they laughed, and they didn't care there was a war. They didn't care about anything. And they sure weren't lonely.

So, you see, parents, sometimes we think our children are just fine. They are in good hands, or so we think. Most of the time, however, we are not alright. Children need education in every area, as much as we can give them, so they will know the dangers, even if THEY think they are safe.

NUMBING THE PAIN

The preceding situation is an unhealthy solution in combating loneliness. Many adolescents will turn to drugs to numb the pain of loneliness. Young adolescents and even older adolescents find it very difficult to put loneliness in its correct perspective. And just what is the correct perspective? We must hang in there until it decides to go away. Growing older, we have more of an access to other ways, such as tranquilizers and alcohol. We need to be aware of their effects.

Here I am drinking again.
Hoping to forget
the things you said
the time I spent
Trying to love you
giving all I had.

Does life go on?
Does life forgive?

Here I am drinking again
Maybe sleep will overpower
the lies
the lonely years!

Your music seemed to quiet the time
Made me forget
who I really was.

I cannot go on living
in your fantasy, my man.
Never again
may I give all.

But yet . . . my heart is so vulnerable
so easily swept away!
Here I am drinking again
trying to forget.

(22 years old)

HEALTHY SOLUTIONS IN COMBATING LONELINESS

There are ways an adolescent can combat loneliness. Sometimes we, as parents, think loneliness is a very natural thing for an adolescent to feel. It is. It is perfectly normal. It's the pits. What can happen with loneliness, however, is that it can very easily slide into depression and on into suicide. You have to remember our hormones are also really doing a number on us. Up and down, up and down. Peer pressure at this age is intense. And who knows? What if there are medical problems we haven't even thought of?

The most important thing a parent can do is to keep communication open. Kids DO want to talk. In fact, the title of this book should be, "Kids Want to Talk." I'll never forget a little friend we had over. She was 12 years old—the perfect student, straight A's, practically a concert pianist, winner in gymnastics. She was watching *Little House on the Prairie* while I was preparing dinner. *Little House on the Prairie* was not one of my favorites, so I wasn't even listening. What was interesting, however, was her concentration on the show. I watched, but I didn't let her know I was watching her. I heard a sniffle, and thought it was a cold. I saw one little tear creep down her cheek.

She looked at me. She knew I had seen. She looked down as if she were ashamed. I sat down to watch the rest of the show with her. I smiled at her, she smiled back and knew it was alright. She continued to cry, and the cries developed into sobs.

Children like company when they're sad. It's okay to be sad. But I could tell she felt stupid for acting like a kid (or that is how I imagined her thoughts). I gave her a hug and she apologized. I reached for her face, held it and said, "Isn't it wonderful to have feelings?" Now she REALLY knew it was alright to cry, and I hugged her.

We sat down and talked about the show for a half an hour after that. You see, it is wonderful we can feel pain or empathy for others. (It had been a story about a girl who had died.) But we need to be so close to our children that we can sense when they are troubled. We need to be right there with them to help them cry. Crying is a release, crying is good. It's alright if we feel bad with them. And when it's over, when we have cried our hearts out, then we talk about it. It helps our children learn there will always be problems, and we can certainly feel bad about them . . ., but there is usually a solution. For one thing, they are not alone.

I worked in a child psych ward. I saw problems with eight-year-olds starting fires. Anorexia in nine-year-olds. Attempted suicides by twelve-year-olds. Right next door to us were fifteen-year-olds burning cigarettes into their hands. Children using their sheets to try to hang themselves. It happened every day!

Lock 'em up! God knows the parents couldn't handle them anymore. Extreme cases were flown in from other states because nothing else could be done. The kids would slap, and spit into the faces of the people trying to help them. They would even urinate on them.

I was 18 years old at the time. I was feeling pretty lonely myself. And all of us had one thing in common. We didn't have anybody. There was a little girl. She was there because she had tried to kill herself. She was 12 years old.

One day she was walking around like a zombie. I called her over. I said, "How are ya doing, Lori?"

"How am I doing?"

"Yeah, I was wondering how you were doing?"

"Fine, I guess." She looked at me suspiciously.

I looked like an adult, so I must have wanted something. She wanted to challenge me. "How do you think I'm doing?" she asked defensively. She thought I would respond by looking at her chart.

"I don't know . . . I thought you looked sad. Are you sad?"

"What do you think, I'm in here, aren't I?"

"Yeah, you're right. I wouldn't feel real hot if I had to be locked up . . . did you really try to kill yourself?"

"Of course I tried to kill myself. I'm still trying to kill myself, but they won't let me. They take everything away."

"It gets pretty lonely out there, doesn't it?" I asked softly.

She looked at me with tears in her eyes and nodded.

"I feel lonely sometimes too."

"You do . . . you really do?" she said in surprise.

I nodded. "When I saw you looking sad, I was wondering what you were feeling or thinking . . ."

"Feeling?"

"You must have feelings when you're feeling sad . . . feelings about a lot of things, it's not just the feeling of being sad . . ."

"You're just like all the rest."

"Maybe . . . but I was just thinking that when I'm sad, I usually don't even know why I'm sad. And I still feel sad. The ONLY way I can tell is by writing things down."

"You write it down?" She thought it was a trap.

"It's just for me to see, if I want to see. Have you ever written a letter? Do you like to write letters?"

"I wrote one about a year ago."

"What if you were to write a letter to yourself?"

She thought I was nuts. "What do you mean, write a letter to myself?"

"Just one try, just for the heck of it. I promise, you'll feel better after you write it. Here's some paper."

She left without saying goodbye. But she took the paper. She came back the next day. "I wrote a letter."

"Did you read it after you wrote it?"

She thought I would demand it from her. "Yes."

"It's interesting, isn't it—the way some things can fall into place? You can even feel sorry for that person who wrote it. Then it makes you feel better that at least one person is feeling sorry for you." We laughed.

"Yeah, it does."

"I brought you a notebook. I write something down every-day . . . nobody else gets to see it, it's just for me."

She liked that. Something just for her, out of her own mind, her own heart. She went on to write over eight pages a day—the little girl who didn't like to write. She even began to show the rest of us what she had written. She wasn't bad. I told her she was great. It was her first step toward her recovery.

I am not saying this is a cure-all. Many things must be taken into consideration. It is, however, a very basic form of therapy. One that should not be overlooked. If we write our feelings down, it helps us to organize ourselves. Helps us organize our own little worlds. We can better fit the pieces of the puzzle into our lives and make them make sense. We can maybe then, tough it out and understand what is going on inside.

MATURING LONELINESS

Here I lie
in lonely seclusion
Paging through my life
looking up lost lovers
Finally admitting
it's not what I need.

They drained me
always asking for all . . .
or nothing.
Words I would say
meaning nothing
but sounding nice.
Maybe they liked to listen
to their rhythm and song.

I stand alone
cold
in the midst of a gale
And to comfort myself
I speak words
that sound nice.

(18 years old)

Through the years of 17 to 24, we discover a new brand of loneliness. This can be so difficult, basically, because we are now on our own. Where we run into trouble is branching off with the opposite sex. During these years we usually feel the need to find a permanent situation. There is a need so strong, that others sometimes think we're crazy. We want to find true happiness in another person. Forget that everything else is happening, like basic survival for one thing. We need to make a statement to the world that someone else wants us or that we are a valuable human being . . . and we will do practically anything in order to prove it. The word "marriage" cannot be erased in our minds. We are obsessed with it.

Being wanted by another human being is fine. But we have another problem here. Nowadays it's almost normal to get divorced. People don't expect marriages to work out. Two out of five existing marriages today, fail. There is no blame. It doesn't matter. Parents can console themselves with their children's divorces by saying, "I knew it wouldn't work out anyway."

But, oh, sometimes we stick it out. Just to prove we're right—that we did the right thing by tying the old knot. We rationalize. Things must be going good, right? Because someone else wants us? And if we are lonely enough . . . we will stay. Even though we are abused.

Sometimes we can't know. There are things that can happen to us. I could have been just fine, by myself. But I had to prove someone could love me. I married him. I wanted to prove my parents were wrong to think I had rushed into it.

I worked hard at the marriage. We were young. Marriage takes years, right? I think he loved me for a year, I really do. Actually, he probably loved me for two. And women can make things so easy. Young women can make things very easy. We have this thing inside of us compelling us to take care of people. It's one of the most wonderful things in the world. We are good at it. Better than anybody. This is why the human race survives.

I really wanted the marriage to work. I had made a committment for life. It meant a lot to me. I was 19 years old. But he loved me. That was what counted.

And I had made such a nice house. Everything was in order. Everything was pleasant to look at. This was my job . . . to make things look nice. We made a good couple. We were pretty people and we were talented. Oh, so talented. But things did not work out.

So much time
So little space.
There was only room for one
And it wasn't me.

I try to understand
Can it be understood?
You say not
I say maybe
Who is right?
Maybe none . . . does it matter?

I say goodbye.
You say hello.
Who has the time anymore?

I gave so much
  for so long
How could you accept?

You say hello.
I say goodbye.
No more . . . no more.

(20 years old)

I knew I was about to face something monumental in my life. I would be alone again. I had failed. I did not realize at the time that it was he who had failed.

Little boy
*   are you ready to play*
with your toys
*   your charades?*
Little boy
*   with a little man within.*

Life was a game you didn't want to win.

I went along
*   as your new sophisticated toy.*
Dashing off to distant places
Not knowing it was a game
*   I wasn't ready to play.*

Little boy with your sophisticated toys
Your happy, hopeless dreams.
Your only satisfaction
*   was when your head was in the clouds*
You are alone
*   you don't have to come down.*
You were above reality
*   responsibility of life*
*   and even me.*

And me . . . I loved you.
Made it possible
for you to continue your foolishness.
Go! Go on! I set you free!
You are free to fly
*   to dream*
*   to fantasize!*
Paint your life within the borders of a frame
you do not realize it is not the same.
Play your music
Dream . . . dream on.

What can I say?
Maybe your dreams will dissipate
Along with your excuses
Your lifetime lies.

I have woken up.
My love had blinded me.
You had drained all that was left of me.
Go, little boy
I have finally realized
I am a woman now
And I must have a man
With maybe just a touch
Of little boy, within.

(21 years old)

It had only been two years. I found myself in court. The divorce court. He didn't even show up. I had gone through two years of physical and emotional abuse. The emotional abuse was worse. It rips you apart every single day . . . and you begin to believe it, whatever it is they are saying to you. You begin to believe you are stupid, fat, ugly and not worth the dirt you sweep up every day. It took me two years after that to be able to believe in myself once again.

Fancy girl
     with eyes of misty wonder
Are you ready
     to go your own way?

Amidst the haste
     and all the waste
Are you for real,
     did you surrender?

Hands reach out grasping
     wanting mystery
     taking your soul.

So easy to surrender, to be taken for granted
Left alone.
You were dead within your soul
You have to fight . . . say no!

You cannot have my life.
It is mine.
I was willing to share
But you cannot have all of me.

(21 years old)

SUICIDE: THE ULTIMATE SOLUTION?

Statistics indicate that a teenager will commit suicide every 90 minutes in the United States. Eighteen teenagers will kill themselves every day, and every hour—57 children will attempt to kill themselves. FIVE HUNDRED THOUSAND ADOLESCENTS WILL TRY TO KILL THEMSELVES EACH YEAR. FIVE THOUSAND WILL SUCCEED.

To understand why this could possibly happen, we must get down to basics. There are probably ten million things I would rather talk about, because I do not want to remember. I am sitting here, a relatively happy human being . . . a very happy human being . . . and I have to force myself. I will have to force myself to think back to when I was 16 years old and tried to kill myself. I was a child, you see. I am an adult now, and I shouldn't have to think of such things.

My parents were very good people. We always sat and discussed things . . . when they wanted to, about what they wanted. They had no idea of what was actually going on in my head. I was sitting in my room (my room was on the lower level of the house). Things had been made very nice for me, I had my own room, my own privacy.

I knew they were asleep. And I wanted to die. It was as simple as that. I did not want tomorrow to come. I was tired of the way things were. And if I was tired of the way things were, there really was only one solution. Death was the answer.

> "And the limb-faced hungry viewers
> Fought to fasten with their eyes
> On the man hung from the trapeze
> Whose fall would satisfy."
>
> Jethro Tull

"So, what in this fail-safe house would kill me? Anything in excess should do the trick. Massive excess. We'll try aspirins. At 300 mg., that should do the trick. If I eat the entire bottle." They were on the top shelf of the linen closet.

I snuck upstairs and got the bottle. It sure looked like it would do the trick. But I would play a record first. Something to get me in the mood for dying.

It was the right thing to do. Everything would be okay after that. I had a sink right next to my room. I had to have water to be able to swallow all the aspirins. I sat on the floor and listened to my record.

I listened to Jethro Tull, a group I had always identified with, they seemed to have a handle on life and what it was all about. I found the music enjoyable. It would have been a good way to end it. All of it. Only the door opened.

I saw my father. I shouted, "What!" He asked me what I was doing. I told him. He made me talk to him. Damn it, I didn't want to talk to him. It would have been so easy. I would have done it in a second, only someone interfered.

I told him every single day was so hard. That school in itself was a struggle, the competition was fierce. I was trying, trying, trying . . . to do the best I could. Trying to fit in was hard. There were so many people and I couldn't understand them. I felt like life was bombarding me, it was finally knocking me down, and I didn't want to have to struggle to get up again. I just wanted to stay down. I wanted to rest and not have to deal with it anymore. What was the purpose?

You say, "But I'm so young. Everything is ahead for me." So what? It doesn't matter that I'm young. I am here, and I am trying so hard. I can fit into whatever you want me to. Fitting into the mold is not difficult. What is so difficult, is to be different. Don't you want me to be different? No, I know you don't.

Travel through life down the middle of the road, you say. Become the mean. But I know inside I am not the mean. You do not know who I am. You think I am a projection of you. Of course, I am. God took these very special things of you and my mother and made them into something unique. Only, I probably, must do things differently. I am this stranger we all must live with. If it's not easy for you . . . then what is it to me?

Yes, I am hard to live with. But what is even harder is living with myself.

Am I lonely? Yes, because I am only one person. And I am scared because there is only one of me. But then again, sometimes I get excited just because there is only one of me. I think it is so wonderful, that maybe my thoughts are thoughts that no one else has even considered . . . what if it were true?

We are alone. We don't realize, however, that we do have company. There is that little light inside of us that keeps us company. But, oh, how we try to kill it. Snuff it out. We throw water on it all the time.

Deadly ways,
wasted plays
It all comes back . . . somehow.
Moving along . . . thinking you're strong
Turn, and you get slapped in the face.

Offer your soul
  or offer your heart
It's all the same in the end.
Play your song right through to the finish
As quickly as it came,
It will soon diminish.

Tell me your secrets,
Oh! Tell me your lies,
You are a twin of your reflection.
Crush a soul . . . hear no more,
You can say what you need and want to hear.

Try for just once to listen to my song
Before I fade quickly into the past
And you will not be able to catch me
This time around.

(16 years old)

There is the possibility we will try to kill ourselves. This, you see, is the easy way out. We know we should go on and fight it out. But we shouldn't have to. It is so easy, all we have to do is swallow a pill to end it. It is easy to know how to die . . . what is hard, is to know how to live.

The adolescent needs an answer to why he should live. They know how beautiful, how ecstatic life is. In the eyes of the adolescent . . . we all have everything one could want. Every single aspect of it. Why then, don't we appreciate it, why don't we love it? Love touches out so simply. It comes so easily. It comes in a smile, in the excitement of realizing it's even there. It does not come by merely reading a book and the knowledge we have felt it for only a second. It comes in living.

Our fears begin at a very early age. A two-year-old cannot distinguish his sleep world from his waking world. To him, they are different entities. When children fall asleep, their safe, awake world does not follow behind; it is left the moment he falls asleep. And what do they feel? Abandonment. My daughter at two years old did not understand the difference between nightie night and goodbye, for to her, she was going away . . . someplace far away from mommy.

Unless we provide our children with a very STRONG, STABILIZED, STRUCTURED environment, things can get out of hand. "But you're so young, and everything is ahead for you." An adolescent has trouble comprehending this. His future to him is tomorrow or next week. And if it is like it was today, they may just say "forget it."

WE DO NOT CHANGE

How can we teach our adolescents that in two years everything will be totally different, but we will continue to have the same adherence towards each other? By extensive communication. By being the example of stability. The adolescent must know no matter what the situation, you are still the same, and he is still the same. What is needed is a communal strength between the two of you. In the case of divorce, death, the marital partner merry-go-round, let him know a permanence does, in fact, exist—if only between the two of you.

> *Summer smiled softly away.*
> *Autumn slipped in with a gentle breeze.*
> *Leaves turned their colors*
> *And with them turned my heart.*
>
> *I saw love so unexpectedly . . . so soft.*
> *You stepped into my life*
> *And with it stole my heart,*
> *So gentle . . . so warm.*
>
> *I was no longer alone.*
> *My smile slowly came back*
> *And I began to see life*
> *Through your eyes.*
>
> *Like a song,*
> *Life was a melody once more . . .*
> *And I saw through your heart*
> *Life was once again.*
>
> *(17 years old)*

It is not only the adolescent who is at risk. Young adults are too. Life is simply not easy. I tried to kill myself at the age of 16. I later went through a rotten marriage. At the age of 23 I found a person who had everything I wanted. The swing was irrational, but we do not see it as that. Because, after having nothing . . . and going into having everything . . . you wonder what is wrong. It is very hard to accept. Women especially, are vulnerable to this. We pick people who are wrong for us, because we think there is something wrong with us.

The second time around I picked someone who was right for me. But other people thought I had picked someone who was wrong. Could I be happy? I picked the relationship apart trying to detect what was wrong. There must be something! I could find nothing. Maybe I could make something up just to satisfy myself. That didn't work either. I finally decided what was wrong; it was me. The following poem was written right before I swallowed a large amount of pills at age 23. Luckily, my husband, then and now, forced me to vomit. I couldn't believe there was actually someone out there who cared whether or not I died. And why he stuck around and saw me through my struggling to find myself once again, I'll never know. Maybe he loved me.

> *Time;*
>
> *Time is all I'm asking*
> *To finish this never ending task*
> *That someday must be done.*
> *To finalize*
>   *this foolish game*
>   *that for once*
>   *must be won.*
>
> *Tell me;*
> *Tell me if the end*
>   *will justify the means.*
> *How much longer*
> *And how many more*
>   *dirty deeds?*
>
> *This ingrown sense*
> *Tells me the end is near*
> *But please . . .*
> *Tell me when and where*
> *It will all adhere.*
> *And will it bring the answer*
> *Hopefully . . .*
> *Oh, so soon.*
>
> *(23 years old)*

The attempt on my life went a little beyond just basic struggling. What made me actually try to do it was because of a simple domestic argument, a basic difference between husband and wife. I think it was the look of disgust in his eyes which finally drove me into it, and this to me represented the end. I could not look beyond the argument. I thought his being angry with me meant he would leave me. I could not comprehend the fact people do argue and do disagree, but they can and do come together once again.

Trying to commit suicide as a young adult is different from trying to kill yourself when you're a teenager. You tend to rationalize. I thought I had fulfilled my purpose in life. Why go on to suffer more? I had saved five lives at that point. Two who were in a motorcycle accident, one suffering from a stroke, a potential suicide, and another I won't describe.

We need more concrete answers during this period in our lives. Where the adolescent can't perceive past a week or two, the young adult can look a year or two down the road, but that is all.

Just as we have to listen to our children, we must listen to ourselves. There is a little voice inside of each one of us, but we usually don't hear it. That's because we aren't listening. If we open ourselves up to hearing it, it will give us the answers. It comes in the form of "thoughts," and I'm glad I finally listened. I finally learned that whatever happened in the world—I had a friend to help pull me through. That friend was me.

WHY DOES THIS HAPPEN?

Young males are more likely to kill themselves. They outnumber women three to one in actual suicides. Suicide attempts, however, are higher among women outnumbering the men three to one.

In talking with a juvenile detective, I was told that the main cause for males killing themselves was due to rejection from a girlfriend or wife. More suicides occur once males are out of high school when they feel pressured into performing, achieving, and accomplishing.

Table 1. Male suicide rates in the United States (per 100,000). *

| | Age Group (Years) | | |
	10–14	15–19	20–24
1950	0.5	3.5	9.3
1960	0.9	5.6	11.5
1970	0.9	8.8	19.3
1975	1.2	12.2	26.4
1977	1.6	14.2	29.9

*Mortality Statistics Branch, National Center for Health Statistics: US Department of Health, Education and Welfare, Vital Statistics of the United States, Volume II, Mortality Part A (published 1960–1970 and 1972–1973; unpublished 1950–59, 1974–75, 1976–77).

**Table 2. Female suicide rates in the United States
(per 100,000).** *

	Age Group (Years)		
	10-14	15-19	20-24
1950	0.1	1.8	3.3
1960	0.2	1.6	2.9
1970	0.3	2.9	5.7
1975	0.4	2.9	6.8
1977	0.5	3.4	7.3

*Mortality Statistics Branch, National Center for Health Statistics: US Department of Health, Education and Welfare, Vital Statistics of the United States, Volume II, Mortality Part A (published 1960–1970 and 1972–1973; unpublished 1950–59, 1974–75, 1976–77).

When finals week arrives on the college campuses, the figures will rise. More deaths occur during the holidays through December, January, and February. However, there are even more deaths in January and February, because elation from the holidays decreases, sending persons into a depressed state of mind.

The police department also noticed a sharp increase in suicides with kids 13 to 14 years of age. In citing the crux of the problem, they blamed it on outside pressure and basic peer pressures. Another interesting observation was that in the case of juvenile crime, the adolescent is more likely to come from a single parent home. Police think it rather unusual to write up a report on juveniles from a two parent home.

In dealing with suicides, however, the detectives did not notice any prominent cause for children committing suicide coming from a one parent home within their community. National statistics do indicate, however, in a nationwide survey of adolescents attempting or actually committing suicide, up to 75 percent do come from a single parent home. In asking what they thought the best solution was, the detectives thought as I did, offer a GOOD, LOVING, STABILIZED home to the adolescent.

WARNING SIGNS

I don't know if I should number these, or just list them. There are a lot of signs. These signs are taken from many sources. Suicides or suicide attempts are more prevalent in the mentally disturbed or in people having a history of schizophrenia. Suicide and suicide attempts are also prevalent in persons with a recent mood change, isolation, secondary depression, poor self-esteem, family problems, alcohol or drug abuse, history of suicide within the family, frequent misjudgement, truancy, inability to concentrate, or anti-social behavior.

There are studies taking place indicating children as young as two or two and a half may actually be committing or are attempting to commit suicide. The children do not perceive the attempt as actually bringing about death, but rather, "wanting to go away." Such cases may be children taking drug overdoses, or jumping in front of cars. Hospitals are now being warned to study drug overdoses or accidents more carefully, looking for any indication.

Suicide or suicide attempts may be brought on by persons who have had a recent rejection or loss of a partner, failure at school, unwanted pregnancy, threat of abuse or abuse itself. Other signs may be sadness, irritability, depression, change of appetite with associated weight loss or gain, change in sleeping patterns, loss of interest, loss of energy or fatigue, feelings of worthlessness and inappropriate guilt, recurring thoughts of death or suicide.

People who are thinking of suicide will usually give a warning signal. They may start giving things away, doctor-shop trying to stock up on bottles of pills. Or they may start talking about how hard life is and complaining.

If you suspect something . . . DON'T IGNORE IT. Talk about it immediately. Seek professional help.

Surprisingly, most parents who find themselves in the midst of a suicide attempt or suicide itself, are very angry. They think it represents shame. It's not directed against the parent, it is directed against the child. The child wants to kill him/herself, not the parent. Even though, they may wish the parent to feel sorry for them . . . wouldn't it be better to give them your interest before they died? YOU HAVE TO FIND OUT THE REASON WHY THEY WANT TO KILL THEMSELVES.

Don't bury it under the rug. If they try once, they'll probably try again . . . if you don't find out the reason WHY. Usually it's for your attention. There has been a breakdown of communication. They need to talk to you.

SOLUTIONS

Between the years 1971 to 1976 there was a 50 percent decrease in suicides attributed to barbiturates. This was due to the reduction of barbiturates given out to patients by physicians. There is also reason to believe suicides will be lower in states that have strict gun control. Suicides in England and Wales decreased due to a change of gas to electricity in homes. The thing is, government can't control suicide, it is up to the families.

The answer to teenaged suicide? Again, once again, you have to talk with young persons. There is a difference between "talking with" and being "talked to." I made a pact with my daughter when she was three years old. I knew she had lied to me. But I didn't want to force the truth from her. The truth had to come from her. It had to be volunteered.

I told her, "Let's make a promise to each other. There will be many times in your life when you will do something, and you will think I will get mad if I find out about it. You won't want to tell me." She nodded.

"But mistakes are alright. We learn from them. Besides, mistakes can usually be fixed, right?"

"Let's promise to each other, that you can tell me anything and I promise I won't get mad. All you have to do is to first say, 'remember our promise,' Okay?"

It is a very tricky promise. It's not because the line is so fine, because the line is actually very well defined. The promise does not have to do with everyday life, but those other things. Those other things can turn out to be: abuse (physical and mental); saying "yes" or "no" to sex; saying "yes" or "no" to drugs; being someplace where you're not supposed to be; being caught in a situation where you are not in control, etc.

Our promise now meant we could talk about anything. Our communication would not be closed no matter what the topic. It meant she knew I would help her with her problems. And, she knew, I would try to understand.

The answer to teenaged suicide is communication and love. Loving them for who they are and understanding their mistakes. There will be times when a child really does feel there is nothing to live for. But what if they knew, that you loved them SO much—that when they felt like this—they would live, if only just for you?

Help them work their problems out. To prevent suicide you have to know what the problem is. You must deal with the whole person and not just the symptoms of suicide.

If you can't handle it by yourself, ask for professional help. Most states have suicide prevention agencies. Your doctor can refer you, your public safety department can refer you, or you can simply call information. Just don't ignore it. It won't go away. The one thing that may just go away . . . is your child.

Make a pact right now. Put this down on paper. Draw up an agreement with your child (make up a buzz word you both will know and understand) that they can tell you anything and you will not hate them. You will help them with their problems, you will understand, and you will STILL love them.

And remember, depression is not something to be afraid of, it is something to take care of immediately. Depressed infants will become depressed children who in turn will become depressed adolescents . . . who will go on to become depressed adults. If you discover this anywhere along the line, it can be dealt with, as long as you take the time to deal with it.

CHAPTER FIVE

Drug Use and Abuse: Fallacies Long Past?

No, I AM afraid it is with us more than ever before. We are a drug culture. We pop a pill to cure everything. Stress is at epidemic proportions, and we will do practically anything to wash it away. Even if it kills us.

I wonder if we really know...what a drug is? We know it can make us feel good, it has the ability to mask what feels bad . . . but what are they, and what are the complications of masking our feelings?

ALCOHOL

I will take it for granted most of us know what alcohol is and what effect it has on us. Which is actually kind of sad. The majority of today's adolescents are drinking. Monthly adolescent consumption of alcohol has declined since 1980 from 72 percent to 66 percent in 1985. Daily drinking is also slightly lower, 4.8 percent. Drinking 5 or more drinks in a row during a two week period has also declined from 41 percent in 1983 to 37 percent in 1985.

Alcohol is definitely a part of culture. One hundred and sixty-four MILLION of us over the age of 12 drink. Not all of these people will be alcoholics . . . there will be some who will be able to drink responsibly. Unfortunately, some is only some.

There is no easy answer to alcohol and the adolescent. Perhaps it must be a combination of many things: education, home responsibility, communication, peer groups, fear, etc., etc.

I stopped at our local public safety department to drop something off one day. I had two kids with me as usual. The kids wanted to see the jail. I thought it would be kind of interesting myself, until we got to the "barf" room. There wasn't anyone actually in our jail, they had been transferred, but I imagined what could happen there as I glanced up at the cameras looking at me.

The "barf" room had a shower in the back, and in the center of the room there was a hole in the floor. I stood looking over the hole cold sober, and I remembered a few times when I could have been picked up for drunk driving. It doesn't take much when you're having fun. You forget you might kill yourself, or more likely, someone else. I could have been the one kneeling over that hole in the floor barfing up my guts. A little degrading I would think. I could just bet my six-year-old would pick up the phone on the first ring, the one phone call I would get to make. "Hi honey . . . Mom's in jail, can you tell Dad?" Even at the age of six she wouldn't think it was real cool.

One day a friend called me in a frantic state. A friend of hers had been picked up for drunk driving. My friend wanted me to do something about it, check into it, write about it—anything. I will write about it. We may think we are glamorous when we are drinking, so clever and pretty, but how much glamour is there kneeling over a "barf" hole in jail or . . .

She had two glasses of champagne. I don't know the size of the glasses, but I will take her word for it—it doesn't matter. She was stopped by the police and given a breathalizer test. To pass the breathalizer test your alcohol level must be within certain limits. Our bodies usually process one ounce of alcohol per hour (on the average). She didn't pass the test. She was put in the squad car and taken to the nearest detox center. She was stripped of her clothes including her underwear. She was put in a room with about thirty men and women. They were not pleasant people, like the ones you meet in church on Sunday, they were the hard-core, the misfits of society. And now she was one of them. This was to be her home for the next two days, and she was absolutely horrified.

It doesn't matter if you have a good attorney or not. You are stuck there if they put you there. Put yourself in her place. How would you feel? Would you feel naked and like you were in a psych ward? I know I would. Just hearing about it was enough for me, and I didn't even want to hear the story. I wanted to pretend it happened to other people, not the people I knew.

The young, gentle, professional woman was shaking inside. Then she suddenly got her period. These are things you don't plan. She began bleeding through the thin gown she was wearing. Embarrassing? It goes beyond embarrassing, it's something you remember in detail for the rest of your life. She was forced to approach a male guard and plead with him to allow her to go the bathroom. And, of course, she didn't have a quarter for a tampon. The guard then proceeded to announce it to the entire room. She had to turn around and face a room of 30 people staring at her with a red blotch of blood on her backside.

The guard finally let her go to the bathroom but at the same time told her she had better stick close to him. This was because she was about to be raped. It is easy under such circumstances to be raped without anyone else even knowing it.

So then you ask yourself, how can these public servants treat a person like that? It is not the Holiday Inn, pal. You don't get to pack an overnight bag. You are in jail, and they don't have to be nice to you. You are a criminal, and they will treat you like one.

The adolescent of today rarely perceives experimentation with drugs and alcohol as a result of peer pressure. When asked why, nine times out of ten he or she will say, "I just wanted to try it." This is not to say experimentation does not resolve indirectly around peer pressure, it probably does. The main conversation upon returning to school on Monday usually consists of "how high I got on the weekend."

And yes, it is a part of our culture. We must begin in the home where adolescents see their parents drinking. The question remains, will they see them using alcohol responsibly? Do their parents come home smashed on the weekends? Have they been driving a car?

The adolescent has a lower tolerance of alcohol than an adult. We must take into consideration they are smaller in size and weigh less than an average adult. Therefore, if the adolescent has ONE drink it will equal an adult having TWO. The adolescent should know he does have a limit. He should know it helps to have food in his stomach so the alcohol can be better absorbed, thus reducing the effect.

And here I am talking about all of this, and I don't have an adolescent yet. Let me just speak for myself on this issue. Let me look at what I will do when my daughter is that age. First, I will talk about drugs. Every drug, what it is, including the impurities. What would she be putting in her body? I will take her to a detox center before she even contemplates trying. She must see for herself. We will walk in and see the building, and find out what it would be like to be picked up. This will happen at the age of twelve. What she would actually have to go through? I will take her to a jail again and have the police explain the procedures of what happens if someone is picked up for drugs or drunk driving.

In regard to school, I will ask a policeman to come into her class, to explain the procedures to the students so that it isn't just her dealing with the consequences. I want her peers to know what it is like too—so they can discuss it. I will ask them to make a mock arrest with one of the students, and let the student tell the class what it felt like afterward.

She and I will walk through the streets of downtown to see the drug addicts for ourselves. I will let them call after us as they lie in the gutters asking us for money. We will not give them any. This is what will kill her. This is what will make the impact. She will not understand why we will not help them.

And she will probably still be curious about drugs. That's okay. But I will also let her know her grandfather was an alcoholic. We will visit treatment centers, we will talk with alcoholics, and let them explain to us what alcohol did to them. I will tell her stories of how her grandfather sold her father's baby carriage in order to pay for gambling and booze. She will feel sorry for her father.

And I will let her know that because her grandfather was an alcoholic . . . there is a good chance she may be one . . . without even drinking. It will not be her fault, but it must be all of us who must pay.

It is not going to be easy. She may still be curious. If she is, after knowing all of this, I will still stand by her. If she wants to take a drink, I want her to do it in front of me, not with friends who will try to prod her on. I want her to be with someone who cares. I will not harass her, and I will not tell her she is bad. I will tell her I love her.

From that moment on I will look for signs of drinking – any staggering, breath mints or sprays, indifference to curfews, lying, etc. I will watch her like a hawk but I will not let her know. And if I do find drugs in her life, we will immediately all be in treatment. We will go through it with her and stand by her side. She will know we love her, and that it is not her fault, but all of ours.

If we do go through treatment, such is life. And if it were to continue, we will deal with that. She will still know we love her, and we will all sacrifice.

You see, I have already thought about it. I am not going to bet that my child won't be tempted. I am going to bet that she will. One must plan the chance their child may get caught up in something they will have no control over. If the one plan doesn't work, then you think of another one. Of course, my hope is that she will never take that first drink, but you must deal in reality. I will try to scare her away from drugs, but I will also warn her in a loving way.

To her, at the age of six, I am explaining why her friend is staying at her grandmothers. Her friend's father is addicted to cocaine. I have explained briefly what cocaine is. I told her having the cocaine is more important to him than having his family. That the cocaine makes him not be himself, and that is why he threatened to kill his wife. It is the family who is the victim, and we must show this family we love them so they know somebody cares. And when Jessica and her friend are together, we will discuss it. We already have, but not to this extent. We will talk about the fear of a six-year-old child who was forced to flee from her bed in the middle of the night. We will share our clothes with them and offer them shelter. I want my child to know what can happen.

You may think my reasoning is idealistic. You bet it is! We can make all the excuses we want, but if we start by thinking idealistically, we have a darn good base. My goal is to get as close to that ideal as possible—not closer to some excuse.

Although in groups where wine or alcohol are drunk at the dinner table such as the Chinese, Italians, and Jews, the alcoholic ratio or problem drinker is relatively low. These groups have instilled a certain tradition in regard to its use for centuries. Their use of alcohol is not looked upon as an adventure, but rather a way of life. Drunkenness is frowned upon and scorned in these societies, and the only connection the adolescent sees with alcohol is responsible use within the family unit.

Our children must realize the consequences of abusive drinking. They must be taught responsible use. They need to know that if they get carried away drinking, it is better to call mom or dad for a ride home rather than accept a ride from someone who appears intoxicated, has been drinking . . . or even driving the family car themselves.

They need to know the legalities involved if they are underage. They need to know: eight out of ten automobile accidents involve a drunk driver or someone who has been drinking. They need to know: each year a conservative estimate for children who are killed by automobiles involves a good 65 percent due to persons who were drunk while driving. And they need to know that two out of ten people who do drink are alcoholics. They need to know: five out of ten people who do drink . . . are problem drinkers.

Parents, make a pact with your children. Adolescents make a pact with your parents. Both of you understand the importance of it. No questions asked, call for a ride. And parents, YOU can even call your children for a ride home. Your kids will understand.

For more information on alcohol and problems it can cause, contact your local Alcoholics Anonymous or AA Al-Anon centers. If you are interested in helping or want more information on drunk driving, contact you local Mothers Against Drunk Drivers (MADD) chapter.

CIGARETTES

Over 145,000,000 people over the age of 12 smoke cigarettes or have tried them. Three hundred and fifty thousand people die each year from diseases associated with cigarette smoking. Cigarette smoking causes lung cancer, heart disease, emphysema, and may complicate pregnancies. Chewing tobacco causes throat and mouth cancer.

I wish someone would have taken me through a cancer ward at age 15. Now, after 17 years of smoking, it probably wouldn't do much good.

You know, people tell us it's bad for us, and that it can and will kill us . . . but we still do it! Why do teenagers do it? Because they're not supposed to, their friends do it, and because it makes us look tough.

Perhaps if we looked at the money it costs us. Let's look at what I've spent so far in my life on smokes. At a dollar fifteen per day (one pack a day, and that's light for an addict), that's $420 a year × 17 years = $7,140. (I could have added an extra room on my house.) If one were to smoke two packs a day that's $840 a year × 17 = $14,280. (That could have been one room added onto my house and a PERFECT one-carat diamond.) Just think for a moment, what that money could have bought you. (Two years of college with all the extras? A brand new car. A down payment on a house. A pretty nice horse.)

If you're an adolescent and do smoke, I want to give you a word of advice. You will not be able to stop later on, but you CAN stop now. This is your only chance. Stop for a week, and save that seven dollars. I want you to think of what that money could buy. What if you were to put that money away? What if you were to save seven dollars a week, and every time you saved $25 — you bought a $50 double EE bond? You can buy them at any bank. That would be approximately every four weeks. That's thirteen $50 EE bonds a year. If you save those 13 bonds for ten years, that's $650 just for that one year! Then you can multiply that $650 each year you don't smoke. That is . . . a lot of money.

What can I say? I smoked to be cool. My parents may have suspected I snuck a cigarette once in a while, but I hid it pretty well. You air yourself out before coming in the house, you stick a piece of gum in your mouth, and you hold your right to privacy so they can't look in your purse.

I didn't think I would get hooked. I was only going to smoke for a year, and then I would stop. I knew I would still have my youth, I will repeat what I wrote in the Sensitive Adolescent section (Chapter Two):

"When someone shoved that first cigarette in my face, I didn't want it. But I took it so they wouldn't laugh at me. It made me choke. My eyes watered. But then, it was only one cigarette.

"They let me get by with puffing it for only so long. Then I had to prove myself worthy of their attention by inhaling. I choked again. 'Then it wasn't just one cigarette, I had to carry a pack around with me so they would know I was serious. I did become serious. I became hooked on them. I took that first cigarette when I was 15 years old. I am now 32 and still smoking. The first cigarettte grew into a habit I can't break, and I know it will kill me. If I ran into that person today who put that first cigarette in my mouth, I would punch them. But then, it was my fault, wasn't it?"

I am not glamorous when I smoke. I can get all dressed up and turn every head in the room, but when I light up a cigarette I feel like I have a wart sticking out of my face. I can even hear them whispering, "She smokes," like I already have a cancer they can catch. I have to ask for a table with smoking in restaurants. I am separated from the non-smokers, and I have to walk all the way into the back. I do not get the best table in the joint anymore. If I am in a lobby and light up a cigarette, people give me dirty looks of disgust, and I put it out. Office buildings are now designated as non-smoking. What if I was looking for a job and I couldn't take the job just because I smoked? When I travel I have to sit in the back of the plane, and the non-smokers give me dirty looks there, too. But then, within a year, they will have banned cigarette smoking on planes altogether. I, in fact, am the only one in my group of friends who smokes. I am in the minority.

You may think you are in the majority at your age, but it will soon change. It will probably affect your life-style, it will affect the job you get, and it most certainly will affect your pocketbook. It will affect your insurance: car insurance, life insurance, house insurance and health insurance. Okay . . . so I'm really realizing how stupid I am. I'm going to give it a try. It is not going to be easy. I'll have to ask my doctor to help me, and I'll tell all my friends. My friends, because they are "good" friends, will help me. They will encourage me and support me, and they will refuse to hand me a cigarette if I ask. I am not looking forward to this . . . THIS will be probably the hardest thing I have ever done, and I know I've done a lot.

COCAINE

I don't know why, but inside my head I think of cocaine and crack as two different things even though they are both cocaine. Maybe it is because crack is considered a new drug, new on the scene. So, bear with me, because we will discuss cocaine in its usual form and then crack, right after.

Before 1914 we put cocaine into beverages such as wine and Coca Cola. It was also used as a local pain killer. Boy, have we come a long way. Now we put it up our noses, smoke it and inject it into our veins.

In 1985, 390,000 people aged 12 to 17 were current cocaine users. Use has, and is continuing, to rise. Twenty-two million people over the age of 12 have used cocaine.

Cocaine is a stimulant which is extracted from coca plant leaves. On the streets it is a white powder that looks like baking soda or baby powder unless it has been tampered with. Then it may be yellow. Coke is usually snorted into the nose but can also be smoked (see crack). When it is snorted it gives a quick high lasting for about an hour. Cocaine is called coke, snow, blow, whiff, snort, nose candy, etc. The snorting of it is called hitting a line, blast, toot, hit, etc.

Cocaine is usually a little chunky (not to be confused with rock) when purchased, so users use a razor blade on a smooth surface to chop it up and refine it. This is usually done on a piece of glass or mirror. Small "lines" representing a "hit" for each nostril are drawn up into the nose with a straw or a dollar bill (snorting). Others may use a coke spoon and lift it up to their nose to snort it. It can also be scooped up into a little fingernail and then snorted.

Cocaine can cause sudden death. Sudden death means there are virtually no warning signs—a victim simply collapses and dies. Cocaine can paralyze the heart muscle. Convulsions from cocaine use can occur at any time without warning.

Cocaine on the streets is not pure and it may be cut with a variety of things such as local anesthetics, stimulants, sugar, baking soda and powder, etc. Many times the cutting agent contains particles and bacteria which can cause an infection throughout the entire body.

A common medical problem with cocaine use is dental. Many times teeth have to be pulled. Malnutrition may occur. Hoarse voices, pneumonia, and replacing or cutting out nose cartilage can happen—it eats right through the nose. When cocaine is injected, infections and diseases can break out: AIDS, hepatitis, Delta Agent and Epstein Barr virus.

Cocaine overdose and cocaine toxicity are life-threatening. They must be treated as an emergency situation and in a hospital. Cocaine use is addicting and many people are willing to give up their families, their jobs and their lives—just for that rush.

There is a certain nervousness in a cocaine user, inability to sit for even short periods of time, agitated behavior, constant sniffling (as with a cold), they may brush their fingers along the bottom of their nose from the irritation. It will seem like they have a lot of energy, and usually they will sound like they have a cold.

Many cocaine users use other drugs besides cocaine because nerves get so raw. Heroin is often used along with valium, quaaludes, barbiturates and alcohol. Addiction to nasal sprays can also occur.

Treatment for cocaine abuse is either in-patient or out-patient, depending upon the severity. Cocaine addiction is both physical and emotional. Usually there is withdrawal.

Every day, at least one ton of cocaine is being ingested, snorted, smoked, injected or eaten in the United States. In 1985 alone, it was believed over 100 tons of cocaine were smuggled into the country. The street product of that amount would be double or triple—200 to 300 tons. Although cocaine is usually thought of in terms of a powder which is snorted through the nose, there is another form, crack, which is more dangerous.

Powder cocaine is very expensive. It costs from $100 to $200 a gram. Some people go through a gram a day, and others a gram a week.

I am at the point in my life where I cannot even count the number of lives I personally know . . . who have been affected by cocaine. I have already told you about my friend who murdered a man. I have already told you about a friend who was strangled to death. Even my hairdresser was put in jail for dealing cocaine. People deal and steal in order to pay for the habit. It's not just the people on the streets, it's in everyday life. In every profession. People who know better, but are willing to sacrifice for a short kick. A short rush to the brain and heart. And they are killing themselves. How many athletes have we lost now? How many more are on it? Plenty. The thing is, there are a lot of other people out there who know what's going on too. It's only a matter of time before they get caught. And then what is the outlook? Prison. One person I know broke his own leg so that he would be separated from the other men in prison. That was how afraid he was of the other men. And if you are on cocaine and your dealer gets caught? You know what your friend will probably do? He'll barter with his prison time. He may just get a shorter sentence because he tells them about you. And then you will get caught, and YOU will be the one in prison. It doesn't matter if you're just doing it for fun. It isn't fun any longer, especially if you sell a little to another friend. Now you're a dealer too.

I don't even know what to say anymore. Maybe you have to watch for yourself how a personality changes, how that person you know or you yourself change into a different person into someone who is paranoid, whose values change, who will now cheat at anything because they are cheating themselves. The thing is, once you get started on it, you have to hit bottom before you realize what you have done. And everything you had, even yourself . . . will be gone. You will not be able to get it back . . . you'll have to start from scratch.

If you or anyone you know is using cocaine or crack, call the National Cocaine Hotline, 1-800-COCAINE to help you or them get off of it. Cocaine can kill you in a second. Now that's what I call a REAL RUSH.

CRACK

So how big is the problem of crack and cocaine? The cocaine hotline is receiving 2,000 calls a day. That's a pretty big problem. Twenty-two million Americans have tried cocaine, 6 million use it twice a month and 2 million are addicted.

A year ago we hadn't even heard of crack. Crack is extracted from powder cocaine, and is put through a chemical process which results in the formulation of tiny chunks or rocks.

Dealers prefer to sell crack because it is cheaper, easier to handle and is more addicting. They can make more money. Crack is almost pure cocaine. It can be crushed, mixed with tobacco and smoked in a cigarette.

What can happen when smoking crack is your system can literally explode at some point through respiratory failure, cerebral hemorrhage, cardiac arrest or epileptic seizure. Crack is a form of cocaine that can cause an immediate lethal dosage within the body. Crack or cocaine is not considered a narcotic, and the medical community seems to be bickering back and forth on what exactly addiction really is. I will say it's addicting. A lot of the experts say if you only smoke crack two times it can lead to addiction.

Crack is more readily available than the powder form of cocaine. Many people say they "fall in love" with crack the first time they use it. Crack-related problems occur six times faster than powder cocaine related problems. Suicide, violent and paranoid behavior are higher with crack users. This may be due to a more severe disruption in the brain chemistry.

Treatment for crack abuse and addiction requires hospitalization. And just how addicting is it? It has been proven that cocaine addicts would prefer cocaine over their family, food, sex, job and friends. Experiments with monkeys indicate the animals would rather have cocaine over food. They would literally die to be high.

Again, if you or anyone you know is using cocaine or crack, you can call the National Cocaine Hotline for advice: 1-800-COCAINE.

MARIJUANA

Sixty-two million people over the age of 12 have used marijuana. In 1985, 2.7 million young people aged 12 to 17 were currently using marijuana (use within 30 days), virtually the same number as used marijuana in 1982, but far less than the 3.9 million that were current marijuana users in 1979.

Marijuana is a hemp plant labeled Cannabis sativa, and its leaves contain the chemical THC (delta-9-tetrahydrocannabinol). Marijuana comes in a leaf form and needs to be dried and crumbled before it can be smoked. Marijuana is usually light brown in color or will be green if it is not yet dried. It is usually purchased by the ounce and is referred to as a lid or a bag. Marijuana is called pot, grass, weed, Mary Jane, rope, dope, etc. The effect of smoking it is referred to as getting stoned, high, bombed, blitzed, wasted, spaced out, etc.

Once a lid is purchased it usually needs to be cleaned. It needs to be cleaned of all the stems and seeds. A popular method of cleaning marijuana is to use a double record album cover, because the seeds and stems settle at the bottom. Strainers and colanders are also used for this purpose. Once it is cleaned it will look like finely ground herbs. Marijuana is usually rolled in the form of a cigarette and smoked. It can also be put into a little pipe. When it is smoked it is usually referred to as "taking a hit." When the user takes a drag, he tries to keep it in the lungs for as long as possible and hold it to increase the effect. It may, however, also be smoked through a pipe or a "bong," i.e., a water pipe. Sometimes the water pipe is filled with wine instead of water. Using a water pipe cuts down on waste and harshness.

A lot of kids nowadays are making profits from marijuana by pre-rolling dope and selling "joints" or "jays" (in cigarette form) during the day at school. The joints usually sell for about a dollar.

The effect of marijuana is similar to that of drinking alcohol except less boisterous. People get "laid back" and relaxed. They may experience a giddy effect, feel silly, have sexual awareness, unsteadiness and poor coordination, feel sleepy or depressed.

Long-term studies now indicate marijuana is dangerous. For certain, it can cause lung cancer. Smoking marijuana creates poor perception and motor coordination. Driving under the influence of marijuana can cause accidents. Mothers who have smoked marijuana during pregnancy have given birth to deformed babies.

Marijuana can also be used in ways other than the rolled cigarette. Sometimes at parties people will make marijuana brownies or put it in other food. The effect is the same, however, it can be more powerful because one doesn't know how much they have ingested. There is no way to judge it. There is also a delayed reaction to the drug, whereas from smoking, the effect only takes a few minutes but if you ingest it, it can take an hour or longer.

THC can also be ingested. It may come in liquid form and is then dropped onto a piece of paper. The person then licks it off the paper. This is much more powerful than smoking a joint. The effect is stronger and it lasts a lot longer.

AMPHETAMINES OR STIMULANTS

Eighteen million people over the age of 12 have used stimulants. Amphetamines are stimulants which cause the heart to beat faster. They can create the feeling of alertness or pleasure. Some amphetamines are Benzedrine (bennies), dextroamphetamine (dexies), and methamphethamine (meth).

The side effects of stimulants are endless, all dangerous and possibly fatal. Many times a speed freak will have to take an "upper" to get going and then take a "downer" to be able to sleep or slow down. Therefore, you can wind up with two addictions. Addiction to stimulants is usually considered psychological.

Speed is normally taken in pill or capsule form; however, it may be injected to give a quicker and longer high. Some people dilute the pill or capsule in order to inject it. There are also others who snort it. "Crystal meth" is also a form of amphetamine that is snorted through the nostrils. Injecting a drug increases your chances of AIDS and hepatitis.

When I was in high school speed was called white crosses (a small white pill with a +), brown and clears, green and clears (greenies) which were in capsule form.

One important observation is when you talk with your child about drugs, you should be knowledgeable on the terminology. Fifteen years ago when I was in high school they tried to teach us about drugs, and stimulants, and they mentioned speed and pep pills. Little did they know practically the entire student body was sitting in front of them just zipping along. Today it seems like it is different, and when schools teach about drugs they at least bring someone in who knows what's going on. That's how it should be.

Someone on stimulants may appear agitated and impatient. It will resemble the appearance of someone using cocaine. Their eyes will be wide open and they will talk faster. They may bounce from one subject to another without reason. They will appear to have a lot of energy. A lot of times kids will take speed in order to cram for exams because it can induce wakefulness for many hours. Although it may keep one up for many hours, after the body is "wasted," the body gets ready to drop from exhaustion. Thoughts are not connected anymore, and attention to detail gets distorted. A lot of times people may have stayed up for two days and learned all the answers for the exam, but when it comes time to take the test, they can't remember anything. It's not worth it. Many times they will crash, that is, sleep, for long periods of time after being on a high.

A lot of times kids use the term "crashing" for just plain going to sleep at night, and this does not mean they have been taking drugs. The term "crash," however, is used for coming down off a high for most drugs. Look for red eyes for stimulants and marijuana.

SEDATIVES, TRANQUILIZERS, DOWNERS

Sedatives are considered "downers" and do the exact opposite of what a stimulant will do. Fifteen million people in the U.S. over the age of 12 have used tranquilizers; twelve million have used sedatives. Sedatives are know as barbiturates and may come in the form of tranquilizers or sleeping pills . . . to "calm us."

Although they are usually taken in pill or capsule form, they may be diluted and injected, the latter increasing the risk of AIDS and hepatitis. What appears to be on the streets today are the more fast-starting, short-time-acting drugs such as seconal, valium, librium, and quaaludes (methaqualone) recently named Meguin and Sopor (known as "soapers").

The effects are quite similar to that of alcohol, and if you see a person on these drugs they may act very "drunk," with loss of muscle coordination, etc.

Quaaludes or "ludes" seem to be very popular at this time with young adults. They feel it heightens their sexual activity or awareness, and many times they will take a lude instead of drinking.

Sedatives are very addicting, and if hooked on them, a person will go through heavy withdrawl symptoms usually needing hospitalization. And of course, driving under the influence of a sedative is very, very dangerous.

HALLUCINOGENS

Thirteen million people over the age of 12 have used hallucinogens. LSD (d-lysergic acid diethylamide) can be synthetically manufactured in chemical laboratories. It can be purchased in pill or capsule form or as a liquid. In liquid form it is dropped onto a piece of paper and is referred to as blotter acid. When a person takes LSD it is known as "dropping acid."

Hallucinogens cause us to hallucinate. When dropping acid it is called going on a "trip" or "tripping." We have no way of knowing what the trip will be, however. Some people claim to have found their soul, while others experience nightmares. One never knows which will occur. A nightmare is known as a bad trip.

While tripping, time is greatly distorted. A minute may seem like five hours. We hear things that aren't there. We see things and our mind distorts them (psychedelic). Some people think they can fly. Or as Timothy Leary put it, "We're on the outside looking in." Tripping can last ten hours or more, and although it is not habit forming, flashbacks can occur at anytime, anywhere.

Tripping can be dangerous because we are not dealing with reality in any form. People can become instantly paranoid and create their own monsters. There really is not a whole lot that can be done while a person is on a trip. You basically have to wait it out. Waiting it out means comforting them, and getting them through their nightmare.

Other hallucinatory drugs are mescaline, which is extracted from the peyote cactus; psilocybin from the psilocybe mushroom; and morning glory seeds. These drugs are considered milder than LSD.

INHALANTS

In 1985 a national study was conducted by the Institute for Social Research at the Univeristy of Michigan. It indicated 17.9 percent of all high school seniors had tried inhalants and that 7.2 percent had used them in the past year.

Usually we don't think of a child using inhalants because these are items we use everyday around the house. Who would think of locking up a bottle of hair spray or styling mousse? Many of us think of inhalants as being the least dangerous in the area of drug abuse. Children are, however, sniffing to get high. Inhalants come in many forms such as hair spray, cleaning fluids, paint thinner, glue, etc.

A short-term effect of using an inhalant is similar to that of the gas you get at the dentist. It may make you feel silly, out of sorts, and it may make you hallucinate. After inhaling, the person usually feels sick to his stomach.

Long-term use of inhalants can cause bone-marrow damage, weight loss, or immediate death from heart irregularities and heart failure.

Inhaling a substance is obviously more dangerous than we think. And obviously, it's a cheap high. It's readily available to us every day if we want it—on our bathroom shelf. If you suspect your child is inhaling any substance, contact your local poison control or emergency room immediately . . . it may very well mean your child's life.

NARCOTICS

Two million people over the age of 12 have used heroin. Included in the narcotic family are the opiates such as heroin, morphine, and codeine. Synthetically made narcotics are methadone and demerol.

Narcotics are both dangerous and physically addicting. The most abused narcotic is heroin, and other drugs are also usually abused by heroin users.

Within the realm of adolescence, heroin most likely will be the last tried or used. The point is, anyone using any of the other drugs will undoubtedly have access to heroin. Persons often want to try new drugs one step at a time: alcohol, marijuana, crack, cocaine, speed, and then perhaps a needle in the vein just to try it out. Surprisingly, of the people I knew who used marijuana on a very regular basis, at least 50 percent went on to the heavier drugs and did inject into their veins.

ANGEL DUST (PCP)

We haven't heard much about PCP lately, perhaps this is because of the wide publicity it received about seven years ago. PCP is a powder which is usually sprinkled on top of marijuana and then rolled to be smoked. Phencyclidine was originally developed for use as an anesthetic and is now only administered to animals because of the bizarre effect it has on humans.

While LSD may bring on a bad trip, PCP is worse. PCP can induce actual violence in a person. Many of the kids using PCP have ended up in mental institutions for life. It brings on a schizophrenia virtually uncontrollable. Once it is inhaled, it is difficult to remove from the system, and many times, there are reoccurrences.

When PCP is sprinkled on top of marijuana it is referred to as being laced. Many times, people smoking it don't know it is there and take it unknowingly. This is a VERY bad drug. Do whatever you can to keep anyone away from it.

CONVERSATIONS WITH A HIGH SCHOOL COUNSELOR

I spoke with a high school counselor who deals with these problems every day. In regard to the high school student, a low estimate would be 10 percent of the student body takes some kind of drug during the school day. Conservatively, 20 percent of the students use some type of drug during the duration of the day. And, 90 percent of the student body takes a drug at least once a week.

The child of today who uses drugs is more sophisticated than the child of ten years ago. The counselor cited a new awareness, as well as a diversification of drugs. The adolescent is mixing his drugs.

The age for drug experimentation grows lower every year. It could easily be said the average age for a child to begin experimenting is now 10 or 11 years old. (I'll start my own drug information sessions earlier.)

The counselor has also observed an ambivalence toward drug use. Smoking a joint to the child of today is likened to drinking a cup of coffee to an adult. It is no longer perceived as strange or bizarre. When marijuana erupted on the scene approximately twenty years ago, there was a different attitude. People smoked marijuana to get "crazy," they wanted relief from anxiety, not relief from life. It was a weekend drug., something for concerts. Today's adolescent fails to acknowledge that drugs have an effect on him. There is a denial of mood changes or mood swings. It is, as a matter of fact, perceived to be the norm.

There is no stereotype of someone who uses drugs, although it may be said that children with drug problems will mainly (60–70 percent) come from a single parent home. Average party fare will consist of alcohol, grass, cocaine and speed—it's your choice—like an hors d'oeuvre tray.

The adolescent of today views the world in a different light. If you are 40 years old you think that if you work hard enough and long enough you will get to where you want to go. The child of today sees parents overworked, ready for a heart attack, with no time for communication. The kids see their parents as having little concern for others, and no time for them. This is not a goal the child would like to attain. They do not want to be like their parents, they would rather get stoned and pretend that life is good.

The counselor makes many attempts to communicate with the parents, and he has observed there is concern when a problem arises. However, he sees a definite lack of enthusiasm to try to rectify the problem. He has also noticed in the rearing of the child, not only is there a lack of time for them, but a lack of enthusiasm toward their growth as well. He sees the family's main concern today as that of money: how much and how far can they get ahead. There is little regard to the question: at whose expense? He thinks it is at the child's expense.

OBSERVATIONS OF A POLICE DEPARTMENT

Surprisingly, the police department's and the counselor's observations were very similar. The basic order in prominence of the various drugs being used today is: alcohol, marijuana, speed, cocaine. Thus, inasmuch as marijuana runs a very close second . . . alcohol remains number one.

How do children even find liquor who are underage? In the same fashion they have been finding it throughout the years. It may be carried under a jacket and out of the house. It may be purchased at a local liquor store with the adolescent leaving an impression he is older than he is. Or perhaps they may inconspicuously linger outside the liquor store waiting for a likely candidate to buy for them. Obviously, there are no problems in availability.

As for locating other various drugs, the dealers are more than "eager to please." However, there is more caution taken today than there was five years ago to whom the dealer will sell to. You must now have a very close "connection."

The police department has also noted an upward trend in the adolescent who has a drinking problem or who is an alcoholic. In commenting on how one midwestern city dealt with the juvenile who drank while driving, their answer was "severely."

The child is not given a ride home into the parent's arms with a little slap on the wrist. On the contrary. He is escorted to a juvenile detoxification center and is treated as if he DOES have a problem and IS a criminal. The police department hopes by dealing with the situation as a "crisis" it will in turn force the parent to become as involved as possible. Their aim is to shock the parent into taking more of a responsibility towards their child.

Once a juvenile is taken to a detox center he is evaluated. It may end up to be a short-term observation, a long-term observation, or may go on to become a "lock-up." It all depends on the individual or the circumstance. Most of these centers are in accord to the county. Where many of the problems arise is in the area of payment to the center itself. Obviously, the treatment center will ask the parent, or in turn, the insurance company to pay. However, there are many instances where the parent will refuse to pay, along with the insurance company's refusal, thus forcing the county (or the taxpayer) to pay. There are even some cases where a police department has had to lay off officers due to a high percentage of children needing detox, therefore, cutting back on spending in other needed areas.

In attempting to understand further, the police department cited one of the main problems of concern they have noticed is a definite lack of parent-child communication. By the time the child has driven a car while intoxicated, or is sitting in juvenile court waiting for his parents to come and bail him out . . . the problem has already been years in the making. Here we are dealing with a parent and a child who have not effectively talked for years. So how do we begin now?

The department has also observed that in the case of the child who uses drugs or alcohol, a good 50–60 percent will come from a single parent home. And in dealing with a criminal act in conjunction with drugs or alcohol the percentage jumps up to 80–90 percent of the children coming from a single parent home.

In regard to what the various problems may be in reference to a child or young adult who is using drugs or alcohol, the most prominent occurrence is vandalism. However, shop-lifting and theft run a close second. In attempting to understand "why," the basic answer appears to be for "kicks." Or perhaps the adolescent had previously thought about stealing a car (or whatever) but had never had the nerve to actually go through with it. Thus, when they were high they felt themselves to be more invincible.

The police department realizes many of these problems may stem from, or be due to, our present economic status. The parents are forced to work longer hours or take a second job in order to "keep up," therefore leaving the child on his own more than ever. So . . . what does the adolescent do in attempting to entertain himself for those long hours? He may very well turn to drugs or alcohol or both. Why not get high for a few hours . . . you might as well get some kicks while killing time. And that is exactly what they are doing: killing time. We need to supply and to have available other interesting resources for them so that they will not begin to view life as a waste of time.

In answer to my question, "What can the parent do if he finds his child taking drugs or alcohol?," the answer was short and to the point.

"Don't fly off the handle."

In many instances where the parent finds marijuana hidden in a drawer, parents will quickly march their child over the the police station, evidence in hand, and cry, "DO SOMETHING!!" However, inasmuch as they do take the time to explain the adverse effects of drug use or alcohol . . . chances are this is not going to have a lasting effect on the adolescent. The cause and effect must come from within the family unit.

The department's advice was not to become overly excited.If you are . . . calm down for a while . . . then approach the situation with a clear and open mind. Sit down and talk reasonably. Chances are, if the parent is reasonable, the child will in turn be reasonable. Don't get into an offensive, defensive game. For then, truly, you will have a problem on your hands. Communicate . . . and try to understand.

So many times when a child is going out for the evening, we shout at them,

"You'd better be home at 11 o'clock! And don't be late!"

We say it with a threat in our voices, and an "or else." When what we really meant to say was,

"I worry about you. It's not your fault I worry, but I worry nonetheless."
"I worry you might hurt yourself or that someone else might try to hurt you."
"I worry not about your driving, but of the creep on the road who may have had a few too many."
"I worry someone might try to take advantage of you."
". . . I care about you."

Why can't we approach the situation on this level more often? Adolescents are very capable of understanding our concern.A little respect on both sides . . . that's all it really takes.

You may be wondering why I have chosen the midwest area of the U.S. to use as an example. Number one is presently I live in the midwest. Number two is I believe the midwest area to be more on the conservative side, more so than either of the coasts.

I realize that on either coast any or every trend I have mentioned thus far will be at a higher level. The midwest area lags behind six months to a year in comparison to either coast.

In the instances of the inner city or either coast, statistics will indicate drugs and alcohol use to be much higher. The circumstances surrounding their use, however, are more intense but similar.

By using the midwest area as an example, I hope to shock you mildly, not astonish you so that the entire concept will appear unfathomable or irreversible, which it is not. There is hope.

PERSONALLY SPEAKING

I think I observed the most drug use and abuse during my young adult years. It was mainly abuse. I graduated from high school when I was 17, and I couldn't wait to be on my own. I had a job, a car, and a place to hang my hat. I could even afford it. I had it made. My main concern at that point in my life was getting to work on time, doing a good job while at work, and having fun. Having fun was why I worked.

I had a roommate who was older than I was. I had friends, but she had more friends than I did. Her friends had black leather jackets and rode motorcycles. Actually, they were pretty nice people. They didn't sit around and discuss life like I liked to, but then they were interesting in their own right.

These were people who did a lot of drugs. It started out with marijuana just to take the "edge off" the day. They would sit around and listen to music. I liked music, and they had some good records. After they mellowed out for a while, they would start snorting coke and speed. That's usually about the time I left. Then they would start drinking.

One day after an all-nighter, I got up for work. There were bodies sprawled across the living room. Even my roommate was in the middle and appeared to be sleeping although her mouth was open and she was drooling. I went into the bathroom to get ready for work. I hadn't really given it a second thought, well, I guess I did, but you live your own life as best you can.

There was blood spattered all over the bathroom walls. It was in the sink and in the bathtub. It was in the bathtub where I was going to wash my hair. I think I screamed. And then my roommate was standing next to me. She was very groggy, but she wanted to know if I was okay.

I asked her what had happened. She looked at me like I was crazy, like I should know and not care. And then I did know. I spotted a tourniquet. They had all been shooting smack. Heroin. Heroin was a little beyond my scope of things and I got very angry. I demanded to know if she had done it and grabbed her arms to look at them. She said she hadn't, she had just snorted heroin. I told her I was going to tell her mother. What else do you do when you're 17? You don't inform the police. You don't even think of informing the police. She promised me it would not happen in the house again. I would live with that promise for another year, because I didn't want to return home and let them know I had failed.

How had I failed? I didn't, but you see it as simply failing to live in another house—like you're not supposed to move, and you pretend everything is peachy and you're doing just fine. You go home for Sunday dinner and don't mention the fact the place where you live is a den of drugs. That's why the rent is so cheap.

There were times when I saw what they did. Some of it was at our house but most of it was across the street. Those were the post-hippy days when people lived together as "families." There were children in those families, and the parents smoked dope in front of them, got their children stoned, gave their dogs alcohol, and shot heroin. And actually, it wasn't really a sign of the times, it was drug abuse at its heaviest.

What can I say? I guess the best word to describe it would be . . . ugly. I watched as they shot dirty needles into arms prickled with black and blue marks. The leftover needle marks were red and inflamed. They expertly flung rubber tourniquets around their arms and pumped their muscles up to find a vein. They applauded each other on the size of their veins, as if they had done something good or won a prize. Then the needle would go in, and the person would breath heavy . . . waiting for the rush to hit them. They drooled through mouths with cracked lips, they stumbled and they fell while the others watched. The others thought it was cool. Sometimes the person urinated in his clothing and vomited. That was considered a great high. Then the "horse" was really doing a number on them. The one thing they never did do was laugh. I never saw anyone having fun while they were on heroin. They sat in the corner by themselves and mumbled inaudible sounds.

In the first edition I wrote about trying to find out what was on the street, that my middle-class suburban attitude shone through my mascara. That I didn't view the stumbling heroin addict any differently than I did the 14-year-old hiding in the bathroom smoking a joint . . . it is all the same in the end. Drugs are drugs, abuse is abuse and dependency is dependency. I still feel that way. But I feel a little differently on wanting to go out on the street to get the information. This time around I find my information from professionals who work with it every day and from medical journals, etc., etc. It is too dangerous out there now. I don't want to go interview my friend in jail who is waiting for his trial. I don't want to know about how many people have died and how they do it. I know how they do it and I don't want to get near it. That is how dangerous it is. I know if I start poking my nose around, there would be a chance I might die, and I'm not ready to go yet.

We are at a very difficult time in history with our drug problem right now. My generation grew up in the drug culture, the illegal drug culture, and I am 32. We will be able to know if our children are doing drugs. This, will be our advantage over the situation. That is not to say we will know how to cope with it better. It's up to us as to what we do about it. But all of this, what it should do, is make us realize the situation the parent of today is in. The parents, as stupid as this may sound, need to be better educated within the realm of illegal drugs. I'm sure if I contacted a police department and asked them to show me, so I could see for myself, an array of drugs . . . they just might do it. They go through training sessions themselves so they know what the different drugs look like, smell like, and the various signs of use. It's worth a try. And then, if you are as educated as you can be, you have to be prepared to deal with what you may find. You have to be willing to take the time to deal with it.

RECOMMENDATIONS

As of the beginning of 1987, there were over 8,000 task forces in the United States designed to help young people in their fight against chemical abuse. You can contact any governmental agency, and they will be able to direct you to the task force nearest you.

The key recommendations listed by the U.S. Department of Education in its report "What Works: Schools Without Drugs," are the following:

PARENTS

- Teach standards of right and wrong and demonstrate these standards by personal example.
- Help children to resist peer pressure by supervising their activities, knowing who their friends are, and being available to talk to them about their interests and problems.
- Be knowledgeable about drugs and the signs of drug use. When symptoms are observed, respond promptly.

SCHOOLS

- Determine the extent and character of drug use and establish a means of monitoring that use regularly.
- Establish clear and specific rules regarding drug use that include strong corrective actions.
- Enforce security policies against drug use fairly and con-

sistently. Implement security measures to eliminate drugs on school premises and at school functions.

- Implement a comprehensive drug prevention curriculum for kindergarten through grade 12, teaching that drug use is dangerous and harmful.
- Reach out to the community for support and assistance in making the school's antidrug program work. Develop arrangements in which school personnel, parents, school boards, law-enforcement officers, treatment organizations and private groups can work together.

STUDENTS

- Learn about the effects of drug use, the reasons why drugs are harmful, and ways to resist pressures to try them.
- Use an understanding of the danger posed by drugs to help other students to resist drugs, persuade those using drugs to seek help, and report those selling drugs to parents and the school principal.

COMMUNITIES

- Help schools fight drugs by providing them with the expertise and financial resources of community groups and agencies.
- Involve local law-enforcement agencies in all aspects of drug prevention: assessment, enforcement and education. The police and courts should have well-established and mutually supportive relationships with the schools.

My recommendation: Always remember that if you have questions about drugs YOU MUST ASK THEM. You don't have to identify yourself if you feel uncomfortable. You can look in the white or yellow pages under government agencies, social organizations, crisis centers, public safety departments, school counselors, etc. The important thing is to ask questions if you have them . . . no one will think you are dumb for asking a question . . . you WILL be dumb if you have a question and DON'T ask it.

And I will add one little thing to the President's antidrug campaign: If someone offers you a drug—JUST SAY NO—you don't even have to say "no thanks."

The National Council on Alcoholism recently set up a toll free number which is a nationwide referral service for drug and alcohol abuse. The number is: 1-800-NCA-CALL.

The Pharmaceutical Manufacturers Association recently made two pamphlets available to the public. The pamphlets depict physical and behavioral characteristics of illegal drugs and also a data chart regarding the effects and characteristics of 25 illegal substances. You may request these pamphlets by writing the Consumer Information Department at 1100 15th St. N.W., Washington, D.C. 20005.

CHAPTER SIX

The Well-Kept Secret

CHILD ABUSE WAS not a subject I originally intended to venture into, to read about, write about, or to try to understand. However, every which way I turned and every paper I picked up denoted gory details of monstrous acts victimizing children. Thus, statistics (inaccurate as they are) indicate it IS and MUST be a topic we need to explore. I literally forced my eyes and heart to at least look into the subject, of course, trying very hard to be as objective as I could. For you see, I, Mrs. Joe Average, a middle-class American, does not even WANT to know such things exist. Let the police and the courts handle the problem. After all, that's what we're paying them for, aren't we? Why should it affect me?

But it does. Because it might happen to me, my family, my daughter, and it may very well happen to you and your family. It is a subject, I, as a responsible citizen must take action against and responsibility for, because it may very well be my neighbor down the street who is actually abusing a child.

There are, basically, three types of abuse towards children: physical abuse (battering), sexual abuse and neglect. Other abuses also seem to fit into these categories; however, we will mainly concern ourselves in the areas of physical and sexual abuse, because they are more pertinent to our subject.

About half or even two-thirds of the abuse cases are never even reported. A pretty "reliable estimate is that there are about 1,000,000 per year. Of these, about 2,000 children die. Two thousand per year . . . six times a day . . . or one child every four hours."[3]

From the years 1981 through 1985, reports on child abuse and neglect have increased 54.9 percent. Sexual abuse toward children in 1981 through 1985 indicate the most dramatic increase. In 1981,

---

[3] "New Light on an Old Problem," 1978, Office of Human Development Services, HEW.

25,677 cases were reported, and in 1985, 70,767 cases were reported. Even the experts in the field disagree, and it appears to be a very controversial issue. However, as much as I would like the entire subject to be totally cut and dry, so to speak, controversy at least stimulates conversation, thus, stimulating and initiating problem solving in this area. Some do agree on certain aspects and study after study has been done. Thus, I perceive the mission of this chapter as perhaps bringing us to a better understanding of what and why the issue exists. An issue and a problem now in epidemic stages, and a problem which needs to be looked at as a PUBLIC HEALTH CONCERN.

First, let us look at who actually abuses their child. Is it that man who was convicted and sentenced to 40 years in prison? Probably. Yet, it could be either you or it could very well be me. It is Mrs. Joe Average and Mr. Joe Average who abuse their children.

In the areas of abuse, many correlating connections can be made. Yet, every case is unique and every case differs because we are dealing with human nature, which certainly continues to remain unique in itself. What usually does cause abuse are circumstances, situations, stress, and our ability or inability to cope with our problems. Many people believe abuse is inherited. If the parents abused their child . . . the child will in turn abuse his children. However, the abuse is not what is inherited, but rather the behavior pattern which was previously learned through the parents and their parents.

WHO ARE THE ABUSERS?

It makes no difference what color we are, what our socioeconomical structure is or if we love our children . . . it happens. Let us just say, there probably is not one parent who wouldn't like to kill or strangle his child at one time or another. I've been there more times than I care to acknowledge. It is normal. However, what does make the one person literally carry this action out has had different circumstances leading up to his behavior than the parent who is able or has learned to refrain.

Let us begin with a man and a woman who may be potential abusers. (We will discuss the child at risk later.) We will call this man and woman, Jack and Sue. Jack came from a home where a stinging belt soon replaced a hand for disciplinary measures. His parents used a belt, because that is how their parents reacted to bad behavior. This is how they had set their limits, so to speak. However, Jack is not such a bad guy, or so he thinks. He came out of it all right in spite of all the little tiffs. He even has the scars to prove it.

Sue came from a home where she wasn't abused physically, but was taught low self-esteem. There was always SOMETHING wrong with her, and she never lived up to her parents' expectations. When she "acted up," she was sent to a boarding school "to teach her a thing or two." Sue thought she was loved (why else would they have spent so much money), but she had never learned what love really is . . . until she met Jack.

Here we have two people who are desperately in love with one another and who really need each other. Sue thinks Jack will be able to fill every single void she ever had, and Jack feels the same towards Sue. They should get along famously. It appears to be a marvelous relationship . . . look at how much they love each other.

Six months pass. A little friction enters into the relationship. Jack is not pulling his share, thinks Sue, and the bum can't even keep a job. Sue is not pulling her weight, thinks Jack. Both are wanting the other to take care of them. The friction gets a little worse, and then they decide to have a baby because this will fulfill Sue's void which Jack can't. Enter child.

A year goes by, and it seems the dumb baby is sick CONSTANTLY. And it always cries. Oh . . . how it cries! This isn't AT ALL what Sue had bargained for. After all, the baby was suppose to fulfill HER wants . . . HER needs.

Jack still isn't any help. Doesn't he realize how much work all this is? Sue isn't any help to Jack. Jack isn't fulfilled sexually anymore, and he is getting very frustrated. And they listen to the damn baby cry, day after day, month after month, and what used to be forced tenderness towards the child develops into a little grabbing. The grabbing gets harder and harder. What Sue meant to be a little spanking leaves a hand print on the baby's bottom. She's mad at herself and she hits a little harder. "Why can't this baby be more of a help to me," cries Sue. A broken rib results from a "fall down the stairs."

Six years have passed. Sue, Jack and little Karen are still together. They seem like such a happy family as seldom as people see them. But Sue and Jack aren't even talking to one another anymore. They are getting by, and that's all that matters.

"Karen is such a pretty little thing . . . looks so much like her mother when Sue was young and still fun," thinks Jack. Jack feels a twinge of guilt as he kisses Karen goodnight. "How can I think that," he says to himself in shame. "She's my child for God's sake!" And he puts his fleeting thought of lust towards Karen away for the time being.

"And little Karen is such a good child, even if we did have to smack her a few times to knock some sense into her. My God . . . she does more than Sue around the house. She brings me anything I want, when I want it. Sue would never take care of me like Karen does."

Jack really loves Karen, and Karen loves her daddy because she is TOLD to.

One night Jack gets drunk. He gets real drunk . . . but not drunk enough not to be able to perform sexually. He feels sorry for himself, and the only one around who really cares . . . is Karen. Sue lies in the other room and listens to what is taking place. Sue is always tired or feeling ill, and she doesn't care anymore. She is beyond caring. And the only one who really cares about her is Karen, even though Karen seems to like Jack better. Let Karen take care of Jack. Karen has learned to survive.

Jack begins to stroke Karen, because he loves her . . . Karen comforts . . . because she cares.

Karen feels loved, ultimately loved for about three years. She doesn't know any better. She has been kept isolated, and then one day she learns the difference. She feels afraid, she feels bitter, she feels totally responsible for what has occurred, and she feels a tremendous amount of guilt. Soon her self-esteem is lowered to nil. She wants out, but she is afraid. She remembers the spankings with the belt.

Finally, after three more years, Karen can't take anymore, and she speaks out. She is placed in a foster home where her previous learned behavior and patterns are not appropriate. In fact, the only way she knows HOW to respond is through sexual innuendos. She is again sexually abused.

By age 16 Karen's guilt has totally engulfed her, and if she's lucky she may someday be able to resolve her guilt.

CHARACTERISTICS OF ABUSING PARENTS

Parents who abuse their children appear to have similar personality characteristics. This is not to say persons with these characteristics will definitely abuse their children; however, these coupled with other factors may very well present a problem.

(1) Abusing parents go through changes too fast and are unable to resolve their problems, therefore, causing or creating a constant readjustment in their lives.

(2) Abusing parents are unable to control minor problems, creating a "life crisis" out of any situation, no matter how small it may appear to others.

(3) Abusing parents want their child to parent them (role-reversal). When the child is unable to respond accordingly . . . abuse may occur.

(4) Abusing parents have trouble accepting responsibility, taking charge and disciplining their children. The only limit setting they know is physical force.

(5) Abusing parents view themselves as losers, yet, they are disgusted by signs of weakness in others.

(6) Abusing parents do not have happy, healthy sexual relations towards one another.

(7) Abusing parents constantly feel under stress.

(8) Most abusing parents are very isolated . . . they often do not vent their feelings, and they do not have many friends.

(9) They have a hard time adjusting and have trouble controlling their actions or taking responsibilty for their actions.

(10) Most abusing parents view their children as having abnormal problems.

(11) Most abusing parents have a basic lack of knowledge in child care and stimulating child growth.

(12) Most abusing parents feel as if there is a competition taking place between the other spouse and the child.

(13) Both parents are equally to blame, not just the abuser. The other parent ALWAYS knows what is occurring but they choose to ignore it and condone the act itself.

(14) Abusing parents love their children.

(15) All abusing parents were deprived in some way or another during their own childhood, not necessarily meaning physical or sexual abuse.

It also appears that personality characteristics of people who batter their children are often quite common among people who sexually abuse their children. In citing a couple of differences, one treatment center suggested that for sexual abusers, there may be misinterpretation involved. (The father thinks his daughter is "coming on to him"). Or of a societal problem where we have instilled a "macho" image onto the man. They also suggested abusers are similar in that each results in a force or a power and that the aggressions surface through different forms or channels.

THE CHILD

"The abused child continues, around and around, learning fewer and fewer skills of interaction. He is 'out of touch' with the world about him; control over his life is lost, actually never gained. What better way to train a child to become a nonentity, functioning in the extremes, than to:

Mute his senses.
Fail to teach him how to get his needs met.
Teach him he is responsible for the actions of others.
Give him little practice in problem solving.
Convince him he cannot trust others.
Show him day after day, that feelings and actions are one and the same."[4]

Are these people monsters? Or are they themselves victims of circumstance? The point is, it can happen to any one of us, and IT IS HAPPENING TO A LOT OF US. Oh, there are many, many theories covering every aspect, and believe me, everyone you talk to has their own idea regarding the entire issue. There are treatment programs where every member of the family must attend (which is a good thing). Many treatment centers take on the problem likening it to that of a chemical dependency. The only difference being it is not a disease but rather an addictive habit or behavior which must be broken. (People will disagree that it is an addictive habit; however, my feelings are that it is an action which has turned into a habit they are unable to control.)

And the child? If the child is young enough, he doesn't even know that it's wrong. If he has survived being beaten while he was young, he has learned to cope. For the moment. Where the extreme damage enters in is down the line . . . on into adolescence.

THE ABUSED ADOLESCENT

"Older children, from latency to adolescence, are more likely to be sexually abused by their caretakers without accompanying physical abuse, although, there may have been physical abuse in earlier years.

"It is the obvious, over-symptomatic expression of seriously disturbed family relationships and has always been preceded by more or less emotional neglect or mistreatment. Parents or other caretakers involved in sexual abuse, are in most ways, quite similar to those

[4]Reprinted from *The Battered Child,* Third Edition, by C. Henry Kempe and Ray E. Helfer, Chapter Three, "Development Deficits Which Limit Interpersonal Skills," p. 48, by Ray E. Helfer, by permission of The University of Chicago Press, ©1968, 1974, 1980 by The University of Chicago.

who are only physically abusive and neglectful and, may at different times express any of these destructive behaviors. They suffer from the same severe lack of self-esteem, have a poorly integrated sense of identity, tend to be somewhat socially isolated, and have a history of emotional deprivation physical abuse, and often very chaotic family lives in their earlier years. As in physical abuse, there is often a history of generational repetition of sexual abuse, especially incest in various forms.

"In addition to the obvious learning from role-modeling which must occur in such family settings, there is also a deeper and compelling identification with the sexually abusive adults known in early childhood. This often gives incest a sort of moral approval in the subculture of some families and is clearly evident when we see a father say with some degree of righteous indignation, 'My father had sex with all my sisters, so why should I not sleep with my daughters?' Mothers also, in identification with their own mothers, seem unable to protect daughters from sexual abuse, and in many instances, condone or actually promote the incestuous relationship between husband and daughter. Both fathers and mothers may righteously justify their incestuous activities by the rationalization that it is best for the child to learn about sex from a loving family member than from 'no-good' peers.

"As in physical abuse, it is not the bodily damage or hurt itself that is most traumatic, but the fact that one was uncared for and misused by the ones to whom one must look for comfort, care, and protection. The resulting ambivalence, lack of trust, and difficulty in human relationships is inevitable and severe."[5]

If the child has not been abused by the time he has reached adolescence, abuse may very well begin at this time. Up to this point the child was easily controlled with a spanking and did what we told him to do. However, how do you give a larger 13-, 14-, or 15-year-old a little spanking for using drugs, bad grades, and repulsive behavior? You don't. We may beat the hell out of him.

Rebellion and curiosity are natural signs of adolescence. It is during this period of growth our little ones are becoming "big people," and we can't control them any longer. Where does the answer lie? I continue to believe within the family unit and communication. Experimentation fine. However, if the child is using drugs on a

[5] Reprinted from *The Battered Child,* Third Edition, by C. Henry Kempe and Ray E. Helfer, Chapter Four, "Psychodynamic Factors in Child Abuse," pp. 73–75, by Brandt Steele, by permission of The University of Chicago Press, ©1968, 1974, 1980 by The University of Chicago.

regular basis, you can't get him to listen to one single word, or he comes back to you with foul language, chances are the absence of communication has been building or simmering for quite some time. We may not have even noticed it through the days, the years . . . it is a very sneaky thing this lack of communication.

Many of the treatment centers begin to receive calls from the adolescent himself during this period of time. In the case of battering the adolescent is less isolated than the younger child, and he knows he wants it to stop.

But yet, here again, fear is instilled within the adolescent, and he must stay within the family and keep his mouth shut for the mere fact he has no place to go. His parents have instilled in him by this time that he is "no-good," and will not be able to make it on his own or fend for himself. So he stays.

INCEST AND ADOLESCENT

"Incest during adolescence is especially traumatic because of the heightened awareness of the adolescent and the active involvement in identity formation and peer group standards. Frigidity, conversion hysteria, promiscuity, phobias, suicide attempts, and psychotic behavior are some of the chronic disabilities one sees in some women who experienced adolescent incest without receiving help. Only in retrospect are these histories obtained many years later . . . the affair never coming to the attention of anyone outside the family.

"But the boys do much worse than the girls! Both mother-son (or grandmother-grandson) and father-son incest leave a boy with such a severe emotional insult that normal emotional growth is blocked. They tend to be severly restricted and may be unable to handle any stress without becoming frankly psychotic. Incest is ruinous for the male, while it can be overcome with or without help by many girls. In general, professionals agreed that early and humane working through of the complex emotions and distorted relationships is curative, while late discovery after serious symptoms have appeared is far less satisfactory. The focus of treatment is the family, but sometimes there really is no functional family, and the youngster must try to build an independent life with sympathetic help from others."[6]

---

[6] Reprinted from *The Battered Child,* Third Edition, by C. Henry Kempe and Ray E. Helfer, Chapter Twelve, "Incest and Other Forms of Sexual Abuse," p. 211, by C. Henry Kempe, by permission of The University of Chicago Press, © 1968, 1974, 1980 by The University of Chicago.

In talking with a child protection agency of a state welfare system, many aspects became evident. In the case of sexual abuse towards girls, who were then placed in a foster home, many times the abuse continued. This occurs because in most cases of sexual abuse the girl knows no other way. She was never taught appropriate sexual behavior. The process of conditioning the child for sexual abuse begins early in infancy, during bathtime, or changing diapers with accompanying fondling, etc. The parents who abuse are also more often than not above average in intelligence.

Penetration usually begins around the age of 7, and if it is carried through until the girl is 17, it usually has gone too far for the adolescent to be treated. In placing her in the foster home, many times the real reason behind the people wanting to take the child is so well hidden that social workers may have a very difficult time differentiating. And even if this was not the original plan of the people in the first place . . . abuse can still occur because of the girl's conditioning; sexual expression is the ONLY form of communication she knows.

Parents who practice incestual behavior usually have friends who do the same. There exists a socio-economical connection between them, and secrecy becomes their main objective.

This agency also cited that in many cases of abuse, one of the more predominant factors was that parents were never taught correct child rearing in the first place. They just didn't know how.

They went a step further and cited an observation that parents abuse their children because they love them. Their expectations become so high that they have difficulty coping when the child fails to meet their needs or what they want to be his accomplishments. Force becomes the only way to initiate or to instill this promise within their children.

Many times in the case of the adolescent who was abused during his childhood, he will display a violent behavior towards others. However, the main beneficiating factor is, by this age he is pretty independent and can be exposed to other various outlets. Through treatment he can begin to learn what correct parenting is all about, hopefully, breaking away from the "cycle." Although in the case of isolated parents and a thoroughly isolated teenager, the pattern is almost sure to develop.

In the case of battering during adolescence, beatings are more likely to be sporadic and less frequent. When a case is reported and a social worker is sent out to the home, usually there is no denial on the part of the parent.

"Sure I beat him! Look at what he did!"

However, they have found that in most cases when abuse does

begin during adolescence, the parent is most eager and more willing to be taught different outlets other than violence. Before, they could only see physical pain as a way of insuring restriction or reason.

HIGH RISK PARENTS AND CHILDREN

High risk parents and high risk children have a potential to abuse or a potential to be abused. This is not to say they WILL abuse or be abused, what this indicates are circumstances that if surrounded by other factors may very well promote abuse. High risk parents (not necessarily in this order) are:

(1) Parents who were forced to marry because of the pregnancy.
(2) Parents who were themselves abused as children.
(3) A mother who didn't want her child in the first place.
(4) A mother who, while pregnant, visualized her child as a "kind of monster," trying to control her life.
(5) Parents with low self-esteem looking to each other to take care of them.
(6) Parents with certain personality traits . . . referring back to common personality traits of abusing parents.

High risk children are children who are:

(1) Premature infants.
(2) Illegitimate children.
(3) Congenitally malformed infants.
(4) Twins.
(5) Children who are frequently ill.
(6) Children conceived during an illness.
(7) Children born to mothers with frequent pregnancies.

Now, assuming these situations exist . . . let's top them off with a little stress . . . or a lot of stress. We have to, again, take into account, abusing parents go through many, many changes and are usually unable to cope with stress appropriately.

Let us suppose these parents also have had to deal with a loss of their spouse or partner through death or a divorce. Or they separate. These situations in themselves cause heartache for any normal person who is able to respond correctly. Or, perhaps, with the economy the way it is, they are fired from their job . . . they have suffered a long illness.

The out-of-work partner finally finds a job but can't get along with his coworkers or his boss . . . then his wife gets pregnant. Their best friend dies in a car accident, and they find themselves remortgaging the house to stay afloat. The wife goes back to work, and then they have to move. The husband or wife may go back to school. So what . . . we ask? A little change never hurt anyone. Nobody but the kids.

Stress . . . we feel it all the time, but how do we react to it? Sometimes I break a few plates. Yes, I do! And what a relief it is! I find old plates for 10¢ a piece, and when the times get rough and I feel PHYSICAL through my frustrations . . . two plates are taken out of the drawer.

AND DO THEY MAKE NOISE?

It's wonderful! I say, "Take that! And that!" They crash and they bang, and I feel RELEASE. My husband will laugh and shake his head at me and then hand me another plate. We will both laugh, and break one together just for the heck of it. Then we both, together clean up the awful mess and yell at one another for MAKING such a mess.

A little silly . . . perhaps . . . but it works. I, personally, wouldn't appear normal or sane to the outside world, were I not able to act a "little crazy" once in a while. I have other outlets, too. However, the important thing is that I have them. We usually do not plan our outlets or outbursts; they surface when and where they need out. Sometimes this may mean against our children, and this is not healthy.

I found it rather interesting myself to learn that premature infants and sick children are high on the list for high risk children. My husband can't see why . . . but I can. I was in labor for two and a half weeks before I gave birth to Jessica. It was not your basic day at the beach, to say the least. Then we went through having our child in an intensive care unit for 76 days. Stress was an everyday occurrence. When she finally came home, things got even worse. She was on a heart monitor which went click, click, click, that is, until she ceased to breathe . . . at least 50 times during a six month period. The colic gave us no rest whatsoever. There was nothing we could do to comfort her. Nothing. The stress level went higher and higher. I wanted to check myself into a hospital and claim insanity. People wouldn't believe me . . . they thought I was joking.

They pitied and they felt for me, but it did not help. One day I finally called my doctor and said, "I think I am going to throw my child out the window, literally!" He listened and believed me. Of course, I did not want to; however, I felt totally overwhelmed and trapped. And I reached out.

I'm average, and I still have these feelings. We all do. The important point is to be able to grasp reality long enough to dial a number. Perhaps of a doctor or a good friend . . . anyone to be able to vent your frustrations. It is not easy admitting to a fleeting thought . . . that we "may" like to harm our child. However, what is even harder is actually GOING THROUGH WITH IT.

DOES THIS AFFECT ME?

You may be thinking to yourself, isn't abuse more in tune with the infant and the child rather than the adolescent? Many times the infant or child is the one abused, and the most dramatic or harshest abuse does occur in children under three years of age. In fact, most deaths occur under one year of age. However, in the case of the adolescent, much of his behavior pattern has already been established by this time, and he might very well be utterly and unconsciously confused in connection to any and every aspect of his life.

In talking with a friend who is a prominent investigative reporter, and who has been specifically studying sexual abuse in children for over six years, many answers came to light. Even though I had read and thought I understood how such acts could take place, I was lacking in a very simple area. He gave me two easy examples of how sexual abuse may occur. And believe it or not, our previously discussed "Show and Tell" game turned out to be the crux of many of the problems.

We will begin by taking the example of, say, a 10- or 11-year-old boy. However, the situation certainly could be taking place earlier in life. We will call him Billy. Billy is becoming aware of his sexuality in a totally different fashion than ever before. He has a natural instinct towards the opposite sex . . . girls. He has a natural curiosity towards these neat little beings, and he can't wait to begin exploring the differences.

However, he senses that in some way this exploring may be very wrong. Mom and Dad make it seem like there is something very wrong, so Billy's adventure and exploration go on in secret. Here we have little Billy and little Sally having a tremendous amount of fun during their play but not really thinking in sexual terms at all. Mother opens the door.

Mother is shocked! She is devastated! She shakes her Billy (to knock some sense into him) and sends little Sally home crying to her mother. Guilt and shame are instilled forever.

"Don't you ever, EVER do that again! Shame on you! You're going straight to hell!"

And Billy loves his mommy so very much and doesn't want to go to hell, and he vows, NEVER, EVER to do that shameful thing ever again. However, Billy IS a sexual human being as we all are. He begins to operate on his sheer WILL POWER and SQUELCHES his natural curiosity towards little Sally. He never DOES do it again.

Billy is older now, and mother has left him during the course of the years. His hormones begin working again just as they did with little Sally. Does Billy come to have a natural feeling towards women his own age at this time? NO, HE DOES NOT. He is still thinking of little Sally and how much fun they had until Mother came along and made him feel so bad about himself. In fact, he finally realizes and recognizes the fact that Mother has been making him feel bad about himself during all these lonely years.

And here we have Billy, now Bill, at age 20 or 30 who never got the chance to explore or to know what sexuality is in a natural, appropriate manner. We now have a sexual abuser or a molester of little girls. He now wants to touch little Sally (now little neighbor girls) not in a curious or simple manner but with lust and fulfillment. Chances are, Bill is overwhelmingly repulsed by the sight of a grown woman's pubic hair, because it represents to him his mother whom he now absolutely despises.

However, had we had a Mama who opened the door with a calm facial expression, saying, "How very interesting. Let's talk about what you were doing and how you felt . . . after you put your clothes on," we may have a totally different situation on our hands. I also might add, Mama sends Sally home in a friendly manner with a quick call to Sally's mother. It is now time for a refresher course in our warnings of what our exploration may lead to.

Yes, I can hear you mothers mumbling in the background like little bees saying "What does she expect us to do . . . offer our virgins to a potential abuser to keep him satisfied?"

It's a good question. As a mother of a daughter, I feel very anxious regarding the entire subject. However, chances are, knowing my Jessica . . . Jessica will be the doctor and Billy will be the assistant. Girls are just as curious as boys, perhaps, even more so. We will discuss sexuality further during the next chapter.

Then let's take Billy's situation one step further. Mama has found him and is again very angry regarding the entire ordeal. Billy is again filled with shame and remorse. But now . . . Billy has found a new friend. An older friend down the block. This friend, an older man, really cares about Billy. Billy is absolutely delighted! He has found someone to go to, who understands him, and who even takes him places. Who wouldn't be happy?

They even take trips together to the Y, have workouts, and afterwards they have a marvelous massage together. They lie on tables next to each other and remark on how wonderful it all feels.

A little time passes, and Billy is over at his friend's house. They talk about things Billy cares about and then talk about the time they spent together at the Y. Wouldn't it feel wonderful to have a massage just like that EVERYDAY? Yes, it would. (Sounds good to me.)

So, the older friend says, "I'll give you a massage just like the one you had at the Y. It will feel good. But, of course, we will have to take our pants off, because that's the way they did it there."

The massage is gentle, warm, soothing . . . Billy feels so nice. Then the hands massage a little firmer, and Billy becomes unknowingly aroused. It seems so natural to have every part of his body rubbed, and without Billy's hardly knowing it . . . he is being masturbated, and he ejaculates.

Does Billy feel shame? No.

His friend says, "It's all right, but we had better not tell Mom or Dad. They just wouldn't understand."

"OK," says Billy.

"But didn't that feel good," asks his friend.

"It sure did," replies Billy.

"Then the next time you can make me feel good."

"OK," says Billy. He really likes his friend.

And now . . . here we have Billy probably doomed to be a homosexual for life . . . or perhaps thinking he is when he isn't.

We all have sexual feelings. In one study with a control group of nonabusing parents, many questions were raised. Here we had normal men and women well adjusted . . . with a fleeting thought once in a while towards their children. This normal man will say in shame, "Yes, once when I was kissing my daughter goodnight, I had just a split second of lust towards her. Boy, did I get out of there fast! It scared me!"

However, this normal man was reacting normally and naturally to his thought process, but knew it wasn't right and controlled his fleeting moment of a strange feeling previously unknown to him.

According to my friend, most incest is done in a gentle and loving manner. However, sexual abuse becomes an addictive behavior. Their life actually begins to mold itself around the behavior just as in chemical dependency. They begin to change their life in order to accommodate the addiction. Instead of a "supposed" business meeting a man may tell his secretary, the man runs home to molest a little one. (It happens all the time.)

Child abuse, whether it be battering or sexual abuse, seems to revolve around the older person or parent's sexuality. This is what needs to be understood. However, we will discuss the adolescent's sexuality further during the next chapter.

If the child has been abused during his earlier years, the adolescent may at this time actually be the one to begin abusing children younger than himself. In talking with a juvenile detective, other aspects regarding this topic came to light.

WHAT DO THE POLICE SEE?

In dealing with child abuse, the most prominent feeling or reaction the police have towards the entire issue is . . . frustration. They feel there is a definite lack or absense within our judicial system. More often than not they are confronted with repeat offenders, and it appears the parents never are or do overcome their problems.

After a case is reported, the parent may be removed from the home, sent to treatment, and the child will be left with the other parent or grandparents. And here we stand in the midst of where it all began.

When the parents are initially approached on the situation, nine times out of ten the reaction is:

"What the hell are you doing here?"

"Is this Nazi Germany or a free country?"

"We deal with our problems in our OWN way!"

"We deal with our problems the same way our parents dealt with us . . . and look at us, we're fine!"

The police department has noticed that in many cases of abuse, the child acts up, is beaten, for the mere want of attention. The child will come right out and say, "This is the only way or time they care about me. When we make up we always get to go out to lunch."

Once a case is reported, many times the child, again, becomes the victim. The child is the one who is questioned in length and in detail. The details do not come from the parents or caretakers. They are very vague with a "he must have fallen down the stairs." Fear, shame, and guilt render the child completely helpless, and the parents blame the child for bringing trouble into their lives. "This never would have happened had it not been for you. You're the entire cause of our unhappiness."

Isolation, again, presents itself as a problem. In rural areas, abuse may go unnoticed . . . until perhaps a teacher picks up on it. But here, we may have a tightly knit community, sticking together dealing with abuse in their own way. Many of these reports come from lower income families when a neighbor will call. The police cite this as a situation where homes are closer together, thus, the shouting and abuse are more easily overheard.

In the case of sexual abuse, it usually crops up in the form of a game with the adult or older person initiating the rules. Many times the adolescent himself is unaware he is being approached. The child doesn't even know what is going on, and it may continue to go on . . . filling the child with fear, shame, and guilt with perhaps him wondering about his own sexuality. It continues until he is strong enough to attempt to break away. However, he usually feels condemned for life.

The police hope that by public awareness, the problem will at least be considered. They operate from a public standpoint. The public has "to get mad enough" to want to do something. The police are the ones to initially approach the situation (if and when a report is called in), they question, and then refer. However, many of their victims turn up again and again, after the parents or caretakers have been "supposedly" treated. And in some cases involving some of the children they have tried to protect again, and again, the next call is expected to be "dead on arrival."

THE ADOLESCENT ABUSER

When I originally contacted the police department, I asked to talk with someone regarding adolescent abuse. Their remark was, "Do you mean the adolescent who has been abused, or an adolescent who is doing the abusing?" The thought had never crossed my mind.

Here lies an area the public never hears about. For you cannot post a child's name who is underage unless he has committed a murder (or something similar) and is being tried as an adult. It appears the more frequent problems surface when the adolescent is babysitting (the most reliable and common way to make a buck at this age). I was shown case after case of 12- or 13-year-olds molesting 2-, 3-, 4- and 5-year-olds.

Many times (obviously) the young child does not even know what is happening. But one thing is for sure, THEY NEVER LIE. Words have to be strung together by the parents in the form of a puzzle, and they may just shrug it off. I have heard terms for ejaculation from children such as "glue squirting," "milk came out," "he peed all over the walls and the bed." Children DO NOT have the capability of making up such comments.

What happens to the cases? A report is made, the report is filed, the parents of the abuser ALWAYS think the other person or the child is lying. If it occurs too many times, the child is sent to treatment, and the parents snub their noses at one another. Nothing gets done, nothing gets said, and the abuser is known as a "problem child."

What has previously occurred in the adolescent's life up to this point? I can't really say because I didn't have access, but a study should be done. One thing I do know and that is the child needs professional help, and the issue needs to be seriously addressed. If we can catch them at 12 or 13 we may be able to straighten out their lives . . . for their sake and for ours.

SOLUTIONS

It seems every expert has a different solution to the problem. There is, however, nothing wrong with this, since out of new ideas may come an answer. There are abuse treatment centers located throughout the United States. For the center nearest you all you have to do is look in the phone book or call Information. And again, government agencies can refer you, as can the public safety department.

There are many ways we can help our children avoid being abducted and abused. Forty-five percent of all child abductions or molestations occur during the months of March and April with the target ages being 10–12. The time during the day abductors look for children are the hours between 3–6 p.m. Both boys and girls will be approached. However, boys usually don't report the attempt because they think their parents will get mad at them. The most common lure used on children is "asking for help or direction."

In sex abuse cases, 70 percent of the abused know who the abuser is. Abductors usually look for children who are playing alone, who look like they won't put up much resistance, and who look sad. Suspects are usually white and 20–30 years of age. The most common vehicle used by abductors is a blue, two-door sedan, because it resembles a police vehicle.

PARENTS NEED TO TEACH THEIR CHILDREN:

- If they are ever abducted, try to get to a phone. Dial 911 and stay where they are so the police can locate them.
- Children should know their full name, address and phone number (the long distance phone number). They should know how to dial 911 and the operator.
- Parents need to teach their children a "secret-code" word to be used if anyone ever tries to pick them up, even if it is someone

they know. The secret code word gives the child "authorization."

- Children should never go into another's home without the parent's permission.
- If a child gets separated from parents, he or she should approach someone in a uniform to ask for assistance. Never wander around in a parking lot. Go to the nearest place of business or where there are people. Once again, they can call 911, and the police will help them.
- Parents should play "what if" games with their children. For instance: "What if we were at a shopping mall and we were separated, what would you do?" or "What if someone approached you to help them?"
- When families are on an outing they should always discuss a meeting place if they are separated. The official assisting the lost person can then reunite them with their families.
- It is always safer when you travel in numbers. The abuser looks for a child who is playing alone or walking alone. Children should never walk to school alone.
- It is inappropriate for an adult to ask a child for directions. Children should never approach a stranger or someone in a car.
- If someone does follow the child or if the child feels threatened in any way, they should *run* to the nearest place where there are other people: into a store or a neighbor's house.
- Parents need to let their children know that they would never ask someone else to pick them up. If there is such a case, use the secret code.
- Children should never tell anyone they are alone, either over the telephone or at the door.
- Children should never answer the door to anyone if they are alone.
- If a child suspects someone trying to enter their house they should call 911 immediately and then call a neighbor.
- Children need to know they can tell their parents if someone asks them to keep a secret or tries to touch them.
- Children need to feel comfortable talking about their private body parts. They need to be taught the difference between "right" touching and "wrong" touching. Never force your child to kiss or hug someone he or she doesn't want to.
- Children should be taught never to accept a gift, money, or candy from a stranger. If someone tries to do this, children should tell their parents immediately.
- Children should never let an unauthorized person take their

picture. The authorization should come from the parent.
- If a stranger or an adult frightens the child, the child should yell, "HELP," as loud as he can, not just scream. Screaming can be confused with too many other things.

PARENTS NEED TO KNOW:

- their child's friends
- not to ever leave a child alone in a car or unattended
- If your child tells you about a person they don't want to be with, find out the reason why.
- Be·involved with your child's activities. Know the person who will be in charge of your child. Find out all you can about that person, and if you can, trade off with other parents so that the one person is not alone with them.
- If someone singles your child out from other children, find out the reason why.
- Fingerprint your children. Have dental records readily available in case you should need them.
- Be aware of changes in your child's behavior or attitude. Always encourage communication. If a child is afraid of something, there is usually a reason behind it. Find out what that reason is.
- Photograph your child at least once a year. If your children are under two years of age, photograph them at least four times a year.
- Don't make your child a target by having him wear clothing with his name on it. Strangers can make it seem like they know your child when they don't. The child may feel like they have an obligation to respond.
- Teach your children that they don't always have to be "ladies and gentlemen." They can say no to an adult if an adult makes them feel uncomfortable. Teach your children to respect their feelings of being uncomfortable and to be able to outwardly respond to these feelings.
- Practice reading license plates and recognizing out-of-state licenses.
- Teach your child what a stranger is. Keep communication open at all times with your child, and stress the fact that not all abductors will be strangers. They may be someone you BOTH know.

REFERRALS

If you are interested in any of the following, contact the National Committee for Prevention of Child Abuse, 332 S. Michigan Ave., Suite 1250, Chicago, Illinois 60604, (312) 663-3520: How to volunteer, other ways to get involved, if you need help, child abuse statistics, literature search, career information, directories of child abuse and related programs, programs for abused children, adoption and foster care, child custody, legal assistance, elder abuser, selected child abuse resources, national organizations, and selected agency resources.

If you are interested in the actual treatment of child abuse, for the abuser and the child, you can contact the American Humane Association at 9725 E. Hampden, Denver, Colorado 80231, (303) 695-0811.

Two more referrals: The Adam Walsh Children's Resource Center 1876 N. University Drive, Suite 306, Ft. Lauderdale, FL 33322. And, the National Center for Missing and Exploited Children: 1-800-843-5678.

CHAPTER SEVEN

Sex Is Only a Three Letter Word

EVERY SINGLE ONE of us is a sexual human being beginning at birth. The mother is shocked and dismayed to see an erection on her two week old baby. Obviously, the baby is not shocked, for to him it is as instantaneous and natural as breathing itself. Little girls discover themselves anytime from birth to two years. Although their apparatus is well hidden, you may be quite sure they will find it nonetheless.

Sexuality is undergoing rapid changes or perhaps even a growing process. I find it especially true with the mothers. I don't know whether this may be because we have had children and NOTHING remains sacred after giving birth, or if we have lived with it for so long it has become "old hat." Whatever the reason, it is a subject both men and women are discussing more openly than ever before.

Today we are discussing our bodies in a way never before possible by the layman. It is a topic discussed on the level of a machine rather than something totally mysterious and unique in itself. Every woman's body works the same, and every man's body works the same. It is time we began realizing this fact. We are getting more comfortable regarding the entire issue, thus, ultimately we will have an effect on our children by our outward attitudes. The adolescent needs to be directed within this matter, and they need to know that they DO NOT STAND ALONE.

THE CHANGING MALE

Well now, let us begin by discussing what changes the male species actually travels through during this time warp. Let us begin with the voice. Ah hummm . . . it cracks, it sputters, and it goes up and down like a squeaky violin. They may think they sound like a broken record . . . and they very well may. The cause . . . hormones.

Hormones are triggering and sending messages to make the voice box larger. They are trying their darnedest to change a little boy into a man in record time . . . no matter what.

EVERYTHING is growing at once. The legs are getting longer and boys may feel they are circus players walking on stilts. Hair begins to grow in places where the sun never shines (most of the time). The chin gets bigger . . . quite a lot to handle for one little boy.

Boys are having a hard time controlling their sexual feelings or actions during early adolescence or even late adolescence, for that matter. For no reason whatsoever, they may get an erection walking down the street just looking at scenery or something of similar nonsexual value. Basically, at this point in growth the boy is very, very embarrassed, but he needs to know his penis can be controlled. However, it may take a while because it is like the baby learning or trying to control his grasp over a rattle. Muscle control . . . it can be done.

Most boys at this age really worry and endlessly wonder about the size of their most private part just as girls wonder about the size of their breasts. It appears perhaps society has instilled this worry onto us . . . we know it should not be, but believe me, we worry nonetheless. I will tell you one thing, and that is grown men continue to worry about the size of their penis. They may not appear to worry . . . but they ARE checking it out. And they think we women are bad! (The price you pay for having a woman write this book, and no, I do not hang out in locker rooms.) It makes no difference what size a penis is, during lovemaking it is the touch, the feeling, and the sensitivity which matter to a woman.

As far as unsuitable erections arising . . . suggest looser clothing . . . it's more comfortable anyway. The boys should know this is totally natural and although they feel as if they are in the spotlight and that EVERYONE is watching, EVERYONE is NOT looking.

Hair begins to grow and pop out from the most unexpected of places, and it is normal to have a little extra grow all over the body. At this moment in time is when Dad and son should have their private meeting in the bathroom (while Mom claims ignorance) in order to learn the art of shaving.

The arms and legs start going to town. They may grow and grow and grow . . . some boys begin growing when they are 12, some when they are 17, and many grow after that. Boys can go through a very hard time with this newness and unfamiliarity, and they really DO NOT like or understand such comments such as, "You're growing like a weed! Look at you!" They don't want to be compared or referred to as a weed. Instead, try comparing them to one of their favorite heros such as a basketball or football star . . . anything but a weed!

I also believe that boys during this age actually may have a harder time adjusting than the girls. I believe this may be because for some reason their growth is comparatively speaking . . . more ignored. After all, who wants to discuss the size of a penis, or how to hide or discourage an erection? I sure don't (I'm glad I have a girl). However, these are all very prominent worries within their minds, embarrassing aspects, and THEY don't want to talk about them EITHER. However, they do want to know, they have to know, and every aspect of their growth must be discussed in detail.

Sometimes we parents may forget to share our own misfortunes. And admit it . . . we've all had them. We say, "Oh, you'll get over it. You'll grow out of it. You're ONLY growing for heaven's sake!" But, ONLY growing to them is a very big deal. It is something they have to live with on a day-to-day basis.

Children love to hear about our embarassments. They want to hear about the time we REALLY BLEW IT, and made complete fools of ourselves. It makes us human. We are not perfect and we did not manage to lunge out of adolescence without a hitch. (I'd like to meet you if you did.) They will laugh, they will snicker, and they will remember us for it for the rest of their lives. Undoubtedly, they will love us for it.

As far as a sex talk goes, I am not going to lecture on how or where it should take place or be done. That is your department. There are hundreds of good books on the subject of how sperm meets egg and little baby makes three. However, what we do need to do is to hold frequent courses on our refreshers. Once we have had our first talk with our child, he may have forgotten an important point, or perhaps now that he is more mature he has a more involved question (Good luck). I, personally, believe our little refreshers should take place at least twice a year or even more often. At this point, we can also discuss how they have grown, changed, or what actually IS taking place within them.

If you are unable to talk with your child, ask a reliable friend who thinks the same as you do, and one whom the child respects. DO NOT RELY ON THE SCHOOLS. Just imagine our little child sitting in a classroom complete with peers . . . is he going to ask about the size of his penis? Highly unlikely. He needs to discuss such things with you. If you have trouble with this, some experts suggest saying unfamiliar words in front of a mirror so that you will be able to come across calm and objective . . . not terrified or embarrassed yourself. And if we don't have all the answers (which most of us don't) check out some good books, because we can all learn together. We always admire someone who has the pride to admit he does not know EVERYTHING.

One other aspect which I think is vitally important, is for the father AND the mother to both discuss sexuality, growing and sex itself on an equal basis of time. Men and women see things differently (that is for sure), and we should give our children the benefit of our combined knowledge . . . or even of our misinformation if such is the case. At least they will know we have tried.

We as a society live by symbols. To a young boy or a man, they also live by symbols. Some symbols may mean how many sexual encounters of the third kind they may have, how fast they can drive a car, how many muscles they can flex, or how many drinks they may be able to down. Whatever the symbols, the young boy or man should hopefully have a few positive ones to live by, and we are the ones to plant the seed within their minds.

When it comes to the opposite sex, boys are both curious and terrified. The female body becomes something new and exciting to them . . . hopefully, not an obsession. Personally, I believe the human body should not be considered a "big deal." It should be considered very natural, and unmysterious. And how the mother reacts to her own body will have an effect on her son.

If the mother slams the door shut to put on her socks or to tie her shoe in privacy . . . the boy will have a problem. Not that I am a nudist by any means, however, privacy should be something which grows gradually. If the boy has never before seen or witnessed a female body, you can be quite sure he will try his darnedest to do just that. And where will he find one? Try a porno magazine, through a peep hole, or window, etc. And he will then be viewing women and girls through exploitive eyes. This is not what women are or what they should be considered.

It all revolves around how the parent views both privacy and himself to determine the boy's attitude towards women. I surely am not suggesting the mother go out of her way to expose herself. It should be something natural which has developed throughout the years. Certainly, she did not hide her breast when her son was an infant in order to nourish him. It was a natural act.

The same goes for the father. This boy will feel very out of place taking showers with the gang after athletics or gym if he has a father who slams the door shut to brush his teeth. The boy will have developed a complex and feel HIS body is something to be hidden or to be ashamed of.

In sharing with you one aspect in regard to sexuality and everything before this point of which we have discussed, we must glance to other cultures other than our own. In visiting with my cousin, who has spent years in Africa, studying and living with other cultures, I have come to notice a vast and decided difference between the family units.

In Africa the family truly lives together, I mean LIVES together. They do not insist a child sleep alone in his own room, nor away from his brothers and sisters. To them this could be considered neglect and in a fashion . . . child abuse. They care for one another in every sense, and are able to take responsibility for themselves and their family. They are more well adjusted emotionally than we will ever be. They are calmer in every respect, and in the realm of sexuality, view the body as a natural entity. They may be lacking in what we perceive to be growth, however, wouldn't it be wonderful to be able to bring the two together? To be able to unite our families within the realm of caring AND responsibility, and have EVERYTHING ELSE working for us?

What boys need at any age is the same as girls. They need to be respected as an individual who has a urgency to grow and to learn. We need to talk with them regarding every aspect. Sensuality, our ability to sense, to touch, and to feel. Sexuality . . . our wants, our lusts, and our desires. The changes going on within our minds . . . the confusion, the misinterpretation, and our anger. Sex itself . . . the act, the love, and the consequences which may develop. We need to be able to listen when they talk, and to guide understandingly.

Many times we may confuse sexuality with sensuality. Things and ways are changing. However, many of us continue to believe the boy should "act like a man," therefore, oppress his feelings and sensitivity. We need to teach the male species how to get "in touch" with themselves and others.

The actual act of sex takes only a few minutes (well . . . alright, a little longer), however, many times we never realize what complete satisfaction our senses can bring us. A simple caressing touch of the cheek in a gentle caring manner is much more loving and sensuous than an abrupt grope down the panties. Our society has a difficult time with love. Sometimes we act like we are machines, but, yet, selfishly want only to satisfy ourselves.

We forget what a light stroke against the arm, skin against skin, feels like. We forget how overwhelming, stimulating, and satisfying it is to smell another person's unique odor. I am not speaking of the repulsive odor of someone who has been on a garlic diet for a week, but of our OWN INDIVIDUAL SMELL.

I love to smell Jessica. Sometimes I think she smells like me, and it reminds me that she contains a portion of MY chemistry. Even her hair is a joy to inhale! Have you ever borrowed a sweater or a coat in order to keep warm, and noticed the pleasant or different smell other than your own which accompanies it? It's wonderful! For you are sensing something unique regarding that person whose coat you have. Even sweat can be nice. Yes! It may be a little stronger than what we usually perceive as a nice smell, however . . . there it is! That chemical that makes up that individual is working and excreting something totally unique.

I guess what I am saying is that we can fulfill ourselves so nicely and completely by appreciating or getting in touch with our wonderful senses. Usually we ignore them. We can't be bothered with them. A simple quick handshake is good enough, rather than lingering a while and feeling that person's callouses which he has worked so hard for . . . or the softness of a pretty woman.

When we touch, we receive RESPONSE. Good response. Not touching is so inbred into us we actually have to go out of our way to touch and to feel. I have to remind myself . . . and I certainly do not do it often enough. If I did, I would find my life much more satisfying. Sometimes I think we are afraid of what response we may actually get. When we touch a person's arm, they MIGHT draw back, but believe me, their curiosity will be stimulated and the next person they come across, more than likely they will venture to try it out. IT'S CATCHING.

And if you would like to get scientific about the subject, studies have been done, and they find that simple touch between human being and human being actually promotes healing of trauma. If touch helps us heal faster physically, you may also be assured it will heal emotionally.

Before we end on the growth of boys and travel on into the lengthy growth in girls, we must discuss one other topic. If you feel you are against reading about such a topic as masturbation . . . I suggest you skip this portion. The only reason I will be discussing it is because it does effect most children and adolescents . . . I promise I will make it short.

MASTURBATION

Hopefully, most boys have learned to respect girls for themselves, and do not view them as sexual objects. These feelings, however, will be very strong at this age. They need an outlet, which has frequently led to masturbation. This is what you do if you don't want to risk catching AIDS, another sexually transmitted disease, get someone pregnant, or use a girl only for her body.

Masturbation is not a topic one usually discusses with one's friends or their parents. It is very private. But I still feel parents and child can talk about it. We don't have to discuss it daily or weekly, but I really feel the parent should let their child know it can be an acceptable activity.

It is perfectly natural. Many children do it. It is natural for them. It's just that you don't do it in front of each other or anybody. You do it alone, and you pick up after yourself. This, of course, is basically for boys. It is normal for young boys to fantasize. There is nothing wrong with it whatsoever, unless their fantasies are of younger children, rape or other violence. But it seems that perhaps it will be the mother who will be the one to come in contact with her son masturbating for the simple fact she is probably the one who does the wash. For these parents, talk to your son. Let him know it is natural. You can, however, gently indicate the approximate location of the washing machine.

Little girls masturbate and so do older girls. What do you do if you don't want to get pregnant, catch a disease, but need satisfaction? Masturbation is an alternative. And nobody has to know.

Masturbation is the same for the girls as it is for the boys. It is a natural act, a private act between you, your mind and your body. It's quite normal if not done excessively or violently.

FROM GIRL TO WOMAN IN ONE EASY STEP?

Far from the truth. There are many, many aspects to discuss within the changes of a young girl's body. It is no wonder we feel so confused with everything, when EVERYTHING is happening so fast. Within the realm of this subject we will be touching upon the following:

- menstruation and accompanying problems
- breasts
- breast self-examination
- general hygiene and infections
- to be or not to be . . . a virgin
- PMS
- pregnancy
- the first pelvic examination

MENSTRUATION

The age to menstruate has been growing lower every year due to nutritional and high health care within the country. A hundred years ago the average age for a girl to menstruate was 17, today it is around 12 years of age or perhaps even as low as 9. And at this point in time, it probably HAS gone as low in age as it will ever get. Therefore, it may be hard for us to keep in mind that every aspect must be discussed earlier in life.

Just in case we need a little refresher on how the woman's body works, we will discuss what actually is taking place . . . sometimes we DO forget and only see it as "that time of the month AGAIN." Once a month (or thereabouts) an egg cell matures in an ovary. (Very rarely there may be two eggs released.) The egg is drawn though a fringy organism at the end of the fallopian tube, and starts down towards the direction of the uterus.

In the meantime, the uterus is preparing to receive the egg and therefore has thickened and contrived a rich cushion of blood for the egg. If the egg has not been fertilized (by a male sperm) the lining or cushion begins breaking up, creating or causing menstruation, a flow of blood out of the uterus, down the vagina for a period of approximately 3–7 days.

As the uterus pushes the blood out during this process, there are little contractions which may be uncomfortable for the woman. This is because there is a release of prostaglandins which cause both the uterus and the bowel to sometimes contract. Some women find the contractions painful; however, there are now medications other than pain killers available to lower the amount of prostaglandins which are released, thus, reducing the contractions. Most girls get by with only aspirin, although a warm water bottle on the tummy, or a hot bath will also help to relax the muscles.

Some girls find themselves bloating or taking on extra water a week or two before their period. This is normal. However, a big weight gain is not. For mild cases, the absence of salt will do the trick. A good note to take regarding the ingestion of any diuretic or water pill, is that it will reduce the potassium within the body system. If you are taking an over-the-counter water pill, eating a banana or two a day will replace the potassium; however, for prescribed diuretics, the doctor should perhaps recommend a potassium supplement. It's advisable to consult a physician.

PREMENSTRUAL SYNDROME

Premenstrual syndrome, known as PMS, affects 90 percent of the women in the world of childbearing age. Forty percent of the women who have PMS have moderate to mild symptoms that can be controlled through diet and exercise. However, 10 percent – an estimated ONE MILLION women in the United States – have severe PMS and are incapacitated by their monthly hormonal swings. There are over 150 symptoms of PMS. Some of the symptoms are: constipation, diarrhea, increased appetite, cravings for sweets or salty food (especially chocolate), weight gain, water retention, acne, bloating, fatigue, depression, irritability, clumsiness, mental confusion, sinus problems, backaches, and insomnia.

Most of the women I know suffer from PMS, and we're all different in our symptoms. Studies have been going on for many years. No one knows for certain what causes PMS. What seems to be the most likely cause for PMS, however, is a deficiency of the hormone progesterone, or a misbalance which can cause the symptoms. Studies indicate there is not sufficient data to link dysmenorrhea (painful cramping) with PMS, although some experts believe there is a link. Some women on birth control pills do get relief from dysmenorrhea; however, there is not enough data to promote its use with persons with PMS. In fact, it is strongly believed that women who have been on the birth control pills for an extended period of years, will actually have increased PMS.

Some doctors prescribe a diuretic or "water pill" which helps the body eliminate excess fluid if the patient is suffering from water retention, bloating and weight gain. It is believed to work by interfering with the production of the hormone responsible for PMS and also gets rid of excess fluid.

Many women are discovering relief from PMS through nutrition and vitamins. Sometimes we think we are getting enough vitamins when we really aren't. It's amazing how much Vitamin C and B6 can be eaten up by stress. Just in case you're interested, always remember to check with your doctor first. Results from vitamin intake will vary with every woman. But it does seem to help me (that is, when I remember to take them).

Some experts believe the body's sugar level is lowered during PMS. They suggest eating six small meals a day: Maintaining the daily caloric intake that will let you keep your weight where you want it, but eating those calories over six meals, rather than two or three. Eat foods high in complex carbohydrates, which are readily turned into blood sugar. Whole-grain breads and cereals, fresh vegetables and beans are rich sources of complex carbohydrates. Eat low-fat sources of protein, such as poultry and fish. It is not necessary to cut red meat out of the diet, just reduce the intake. And reducing sodium intake (salt). Processed foods are especially high in sodium.

PMS can be very complicated to treat and sometimes it may take quite a while to get it under control. Many physicians are now withdrawing their recommendation to treat women with progesterone rectal suppositories; however, if PMS is very severe, women will find relief from it. Most physicians recommend reducing sugar intake, all caffeine related products, reducing stress levels and increasing exercise. They cite exercise as being the most important factor in relieving PMS.

Many feel there is a definite connection between psychological interactions and PMS. For instance, how would one react to a problem if they had not slept for three days? Would they cope with the same problem in the same way if they had had a good night's sleep? Of course not. PMS magnifies stress, and part of the answer seems to lie in how we cope with our problems.

Most cities in the U.S. have PMS clinics. And, of course, one should always confide in her doctor when one has a medical problem. PMS is a medical problem and all doctors should be sensitive to a PMS patient. If your doctor does not think PMS is a medical problem to be rectified, maybe you should find a doctor who does. Your doctor can also refer you to the nearest PMS clinic.

Many women with PMS find relief by documenting their cycles. After two or three months of writing down what happens every day of the month, most likely, you will have an indication of what will follow in future cycles. Remember, what to look for is a correlation of symptoms during that two-week period before menstruation. If the symptoms occur at other times, or if the symptoms do not go away at the onset of menstrual flow, make sure you check it out with your doctor. By documenting the cycle, at least we will know when it will hit us, and we can be better prepared. I warn all of my close friends that when the time comes, not to hold me accountable for what I may say or do. I've even thought of putting my family up in a hotel for a week. Just kidding. However, one study indicated 84 percent of all crimes committed by women occurred during the PMS period, or two weeks before menstruation. See? It's not just in our heads anymore. It is REAL.

I wish I could say there is a pat answer to PMS. But there isn't. Personally, I'm not even satisfied with what I just wrote. I want a pill I can take to get rid of it. What do we do, grin and bear it? I guess we've done just that for centuries, eh? Well, the one sure thing we can look forward to is that they will continue to research the problem.

REFERRALS

For updates on PMS and/or research, the American College of Obstetricians and Gynecologists prints patient educational pamphlets. The address is: The American College of Obstetricians and Gynelcologists, 600 Maryland Avenue, SW, Suite 300 East, Washington, DC 20024-2588.

TOXIC SHOCK SYNDROME

Five years ago TSS, or toxic shock syndrome, was more prevalent.

Toxic shock syndrome has been found in both men and women; however, it was more associated with females because of the belief tampons were the cause. All U.S. tampon manufacturers therefore took all super absorbent tampons off the market. It was believed that women wore the super absorbent tampons longer than regular tampons. A tampon, if left in the vagina for more than four hours at a time, can promote an extra growth of bacteria which may cause TSS. The contraceptive sponge has also been associated with toxic shock syndrome, although more data are needed.

Some of the symptoms of toxic shock syndrome are high fever, vomiting, diarrhea and a light rash covering the body that may peel off. Although it would appear TSS is not something we really have to worry about, it can be a reminder to change tampons frequently, use sanitary napkins when feasible and to wear only a sanitary napkin at night. If any of the symptoms should occur, seek medical help immediately.

BREASTS

Everyone has them . . . only the size will vary. To some men and women breasts represent a symbol of womanhood. This symbolism can be carried to extremes.

Some girls will begin developing breasts at age 9, some at age 17, and it will vary with every individual. Some women grow until they are 25. Only one thing is for certain and that is almost every woman wishes she had other than what she does have. Large breasted women wish they had smaller. Smaller breasted women wish they had larger. It doesn't matter. What does matter is that you or the adolescent does not flaunt them, and think that breasts are a way of insuring prosperity or happiness. The mind and the beauty of a living spirit are what will pull you through in this world. Excercise these things . . . not your breasts, attempting to make them larger.

BREAST SELF-EXAMINATION

Breast cancer is highly unlikely in young girls. However, I feel as soon as the breasts have begun developing is a good time to at least learn how to do a monthly self-examination. If anything, it will be a good habit to get into. Early detection is a sure way to prevent or halt breast cancer, and most women who do have breast cancer, have found it themselves.

Self-examination is very easy to do, and it will only take 5 minutes out of the month to have control over the situation for an entire life.

(1) Stand up straight in front of the mirror with the arms down at

the sides to see if there has been a change in size or shape. Look to see if there are any puckers or dimples. Press each nipple to detect any discharge.

(2) Raise the arms above the head to detect if there are any changes since the last time the breasts were checked. What we will be looking for are any lumps or thickening.

(3) Lie down and place a pillow under the left shoulder and place the left hand under the head. Hold the right hand flat, and feel the breast with tiny pressing circles. Feel from the top down to the nipples. Then continue to the inside and then the bottom. At the bottom, there will be a ridge of firm flesh.

(4) Place the left arm down at its side and continue to do the same on the outside of the breast beginning under the armpit.

(5) Then check the other breast.

Most women do have lumps, usually being soft and pliable. Some women will find a little hard lump which doesn't move when gently pressed or pushed. This should be checked with a doctor. And if there are ANY questions, you should ask your doctor.

GENERAL HYGIENE AND INFECTIONS

There is no way we can keep completely clean. Our bodies are constantly producing bacteria. It is the bacteria, when it is all in balance, that helps to keep us healthy. Women will find it harder to keep cleaner than men, because their sexual parts are hidden and there are extra folds which will always be moist no matter how hard we try to keep them clean.

Most homes are equipped with a shower, and taking a shower takes about 5 minutes out of the day. There is no reason why we can't at least take a daily shower, especially during our menstrual periods when there may be an extra odor. The body is a finely tuned machine, and we need to keep it in good shape.

Besides menstrual periods, there are other aspects which come to light in regard to cleanliness. Women seem to confine their bodies more than men. Most women wear nylon panties which don't "breathe." They wear pantyhose, maybe a girdle, tight pants or jeans. Tight clothing causes you to perspire more in the private areas. Feminine hygiene deodorants may hide an odor, but what they usually do is upset our delicate balance. They usually cause us infections.

Which brings us to vaginal infections. Sometimes when we take an antibiotic or are on the birth control pill, this may cause an upset within the vagina. Deodorant soaps and bubble baths have been known to cause infections. Most discharges from the vaginal area are normal. However, they are not normal if they are thick, itch or burn. The most common infection for girls is a yeast infection. This is caused when there is a misbalance or an overgrowth of yeast in the vagina. Yeast infections do not necessarily mean you have had sex. Mothers need to remember this when talking with their daughters.

YEAST INFECTIONS, CANDIDA ALBICANS OR CANDIDIASIS

Recent studies have indicated that common signals or symptoms of candida overgrowth may be the following:

GASTROINTESTINAL TRACT: Chronic heartburn, Gastritis, Colitis, Distension and bloating, Gas, Constipation, Diarrhea.

CENTRAL NERVOUS SYSTEM: Headaches, Depression, Lethargy, Agitation, Hyperirritability, Memory Loss, Inability to concentrate.

"ALLERGIC SYMPTOMS:" Hay fever, Sinusitis, Earaches, Hives, Asthma, Food and chemical sensitivities.

GENITOURINARY TRACT: Yeast vaginitis, Menstrual irregularities, Cramping, Endometriosis, Cystitis, Urethritis, Kidney and bladder infections.

GENERALIZED: Fatigue, Joint pains and stiffness, Cold hands and feet, Increased body hair, Numbness and tingling, Food cravings, Loss of libido, Acne, Premenstrual tension.

Candidiasis is not a sexually transmitted disease, although it can be spread sexually. Candida Albicans is a single-cell fungus. This yeast normally lives on the mucous membranes of the intestines/digestive tract and the vagina, as do billions of other "friendly" germs. Studies have indicated that the presence of the yeast/fungus "Candida Albicans" exists in practically 100 percent of the population. What causes the symptoms is a microflora imbalance (or Candidiasis).

The primary causes of a microflora imbalance (or Candidiasis) are:

- widespread use of broad spectrum antibiotics in both animals and people
- high-beef, high-fat, low-fiber, high-sugar diets of western society
- use of birth control pills, cortisone, cortisone-like drugs and immunosuppressant drugs

Some of the symptoms of Candidiasis have been likened to some of the symptoms of PMS. There are experts in this field who believe stronger treatment (or prolonged treatment) is necessary to combat the more severe form of Candidiasis, which is not only the common yeast infection of the vagina, but is also said to be present in the blood stream.

To diagnose this form of Candidiasis, a doctor must take a blood sample. And to treat this, if it is diagnosed, most patients are usually put on first a fast, then a yeast-free diet with special medication.

To reduce the potential of spreading Candidiasis it is recommended to wash the genital area after sexual contact and to use a condom.

As always, if the symptoms present themselves to you, consult your physician.

Bladder infections, or cystitis, are very common in women and can be very painful. There are a number of reasons why a bladder infection can occur, and it is best to check with a doctor. And once again, mothers, it doesn't mean your daughter has been having sex. Just get her into the doctor for medication. A few ways that may help alleviate a potential problem with cystitis is to drink plenty of water, urinate when you have to, and wash the genital area after lovemaking. The symptoms of a bladder infection are feeling like you have to urinate, burning sensation or pain when you do urinate, pain in the stomach area, and urine that is discolored.

PREGNANCY

Four out of 10 teenaged girls will become pregnant before leaving their teens. More than 680,000 adolescents will find themselves pregnant and unmarried each year.

There are two ways not to become pregnant: abstinence and using contraceptives. Abstinence doesn't seem to be working that well. Surprisingly, the majority of parents with teenagers who become pregnant, did not know their daughter was sexually active until they discovered their daughter was pregnant. Early intervention and education must be the answer. We must begin our sex talks at a very early age, and we must continue them on a regular basis. We must be very thorough in our information. Once is not enough . . . but it can be enough to become pregnant.

Having a child when you are under the age of 16 can be very dangerous. There can be many medical complications that can occur with the pregnancy. It is very important that when someone is this young and they are pregnant, they seek medical, prenatal care immediately. They cannot hold off and pretend it isn't happening. They must seek advice and medical attention for their own sake as well as their child's.

Many of the teenagers who become pregnant do not seek medical attention for the mere fact they do not know they are pregnant. I will never forget a day in the emergency room. A young girl was brought in by her parents with the complaint of abdominal pain. The parents thought it was appendicitis. Their daughter was very large in build, very tall, and very heavy.

One of the nurses situated the girl in a private exam room. It was always routine for abdominal pain in women to do a gyn exam to be able to rule out any problems there. The nurse peeked her head out the door and practically yelped for help. A baby's head was beginning to crown. Labor and delivery were notified immediately, and shortly thereafter, a 10-pound baby was born. Yes, everyone was surprised.

Perhaps this can be a lesson for us, that when we are giving our sex talks, to include all the facts. The symptoms of pregnancy may include: missing a period, morning sickness (not necessarily in the morning), nausea and vomiting, sudden dizziness, tenderness in the breats and breast enlargement, nipples turning a darker color, and having to urinate more often than usual.

One other point we should bring up is that when a girl first begins to menstruate, she most likely will not be regular. She may miss a few periods. Sometimes she may have a period but not ovulate. She may have cramping, but not a period. All of these aspects are likely; however, if she is ovulating and has had sexual intercourse and then misses a period, she may very well be pregnant. If this does occur, you should contact your doctor as soon as possible.

THE FIRST PELVIC EXAM

It is debatable when a girl should have her first pelvic exam. Usually the first exam occurs when a problem arises, perhaps, due to severe cramping. Here again, there is something which can be done regarding cramping and the best solution is to see a physician. The majority of women DO NOT have problems, but some DO.

Since it is the mother who will probably take the child to the exam, and who does know what actually takes place . . . she should go over the visit in detail so that the girl knows exactly what to expect. Only saying, "The doctor is going to take a peek at you," will not be acceptable.

A pelvic examination is painless although there may be accompanying discomfort (nobody says you have to LIKE it . . . I still don't . . . and never will). The most uncomfortable part is when the doctor has to look and probe into your most private parts. But believe me, they do not look and probe sexually, for to them it is only another part of the body which has to function correctly, which may have problems, and they are there to fix.

The entire ordeal is rather embarrassing. However, it must be remembered that the doctor IS NOT embarrassed . . . all women have the same parts and nothing is new about any of it.

So . . . we have discussed many aspects of the female body, many more than the male. This is because women seem to have more problems with the actual functioning of their bodies, and because menstruation occurs we need to know more and need to know what actually takes place.

PHYSICAL CHANGES

What we appear as during our adolescent years, is not what we will look like ten years down the line. The basics are there, however, you would be amazed at "what will come out in the wash." That skinny girl with straggly hair just may turn out to be a top fashion model. The boy, whose legs were too long for the rest of his body, may just turn out to be a million dollar a year basketball star. The fat ones will lose weight. All the teenagers who thought they were a "really big deal," never accomplish what they think they are capable of. The quiet and plain people, who have sat back and observed the chaos for years, will take on the world by STORM, but will have kept a touch of sensitivity within themselves. It really is amazing what can happen! There is hope . . . believe me!

What happens . . . is you learn to develop your assets and attributes and downplay your, perhaps, unattractive aspects. It just takes a few years . . . that's all. However, we must realize that there does lie an unlimited potential in what we are capable of, and we must see to it that we take care of what we do have.

One of the more common problems during adolescence is pimples. Yes, PIMPLES. The hormones which make the body change also make the pores in the skin grow larger and excrete extra oil. Thus, the old pimple. Keeping clean is the best way to counteract pimples. Cleanliness, sunshine, and exercise will help. Pimples are not to be picked, because if they are, they will leave a scar. A scar which may remain the rest of our lives. If the pimples are really bad, a doctor may prescribe a medication to reduce the acne (a regular doctor or one that specializes in skin care). There is a new drug on the market for severe cases of acne. It is manufactured by the Roche Company and it is Isotretinoin or Accutane. It comes in three different strengths and is usually prescribed to be used twice daily. It is basically used for cystic acne and is quite expensive. A fifty day supply, on the average, costs $200. One other medication for acne, available only by prescription is Retin-A, a derivative of Vitamin A. It comes in a cream or gel and is manufactured by the Ortho Company. It comes in a 20 gram tube and the approximate cost is $20, and will last about one month with average use.

We must also remember that keeping our hair clean and having clean bed sheets, washing our face often (not scrubbing it off), and keeping our hands away from our face will help, too.

HOW UGLY WAS I?

At this point in the chapter is where I leap in and tell you how ugly I was while growing up. It seemed EVERYTHING was wrong with me. I was taller than the boys. I was overweight . . . just barely out of chubby sizes, had no breasts, had hairy legs (which we already know about), and many pimples. What a mess! It was enough to depress anyone or drive a person mad!

All I could barely manage was to muddle through each existing day . . . a day at a time. The boys made fun of me for not having breasts. I had remarks directed towards me such as, "She's got a buried treasure . . . yeah, a sunken CHEST!" Every single day there would be something new to pick on . . . I was not spared one day out of the year.

Then another pimple would unexpectedly crop up right in the middle of my nose creating a new topic for the day. Yes, adolescence certainly IS a real fun time. (I wish I could go through it again.) I slumped my shoulders to appear shorter than I actually was. All that accomplished was bad posture for the time being. I tried to cover pimples with makeup, but all that did was make the problem worse than it already was by clogging my pores. I tried every medication on the open market and was tempted to try the black market. My body kept getting taller and with it my chest kept getting flatter . . . which I did not think would be possible. What do you do? You learn to live with it, and do the best you can.

Around the age of 17, the freckles began to disappear along with the pimples. I can remember standing in front of the mirror a year earlier and trying to imagine what it would be like to have a clear face. My baby fat began to shed itself . . . pound by pound, and I discovered I actually had BONES underneath it all. I was beginning to blossom . . . although the chest never DID catch on or catch up. What I had done, however, was work with what I did have at the time. I had nice eyes . . . or so people had told me, and I accented them as a feature. I had artistic hands, and I played flute, piano, and guitar. I had a good mind, so I began to read and read as much as I could . . . not realizing I might be learning in the process. I may not have read textbooks, but I read what I wanted to know, and was interested in.

By the time I reached 22, I had accomplished almost all of what I had ever wanted to do or had set out to do. I began resetting my goals. I unknowingly shed another 20 pounds, chopped off my hair and discovered there was a FACE underneath. In still hurting a little from the remarks during adolescence, I took up modeling, not knowing one thing about it . . . but proved to myself you can be what you want to be. If there exists a possible avenue . . . it can be done. YOU CAN DO IT.

The irony of the entire ordeal was photographers wanted me for my skin . . . the skin which had only recently been filled with freckles and pimples! I modeled hands, nails, top fashions for women, hair, eyes, eye brows, shoes, jewelry, . . . you name it. (Well, not EVERY-THING.) I danced in choreographed fashion shows. I modeled regularly on a television talk show. And the one thing I learned was . . . I wasn't that bad. And we aren't!

The point is not the story of the ugly duckling, but rather everything works itself out . . . we change and we can work with what we DO have whether it be a mathematical mind or nice nails. But we have to WORK with it . . . work HARD, and TRY. It all comes together by our EFFORT.

BIRTH CONTROL

Birth control can be a very controversial issue. It's not something we really want to talk to our children about, because if we do, we will think they will become or are sexually active. In our house, sex is an open topic, and if there are questions, they get answered. It doesn't matter how old you are, the facts should always be presented correctly. I might also add, that there have been other children besides my own daughter who have asked me questions. I answer them as best I can according to the age level or understanding. For one thing, we have this little chair in our house. I didn't buy it, it came with my husband when we got married. It's a "birthing" chair of all things. Obviously, it's an antique, an antique that I really don't know what to do with. So it sits in our hall. It's an odd-looking chair and spurs a lot of questions. So we talk about childbirth and the effect gravity has on the female when she's delivering. My husband and I are both art lovers. One form of art my husband particularly likes is the female body. It's not like we're displaying Playboy pictures, but there are some nudes; and not graphic, just the shape. The kids really get a kick out of those. At first when they walk into the house there is a lot of pointing (if they have not been in our house before). My six-year-old explains to them that it is art, and the objects or pictures are just different forms of the human body, and isn't it beautiful? I usually overhear them, so I join in on the conversation. They are embarrassed. I tell them I really liked how the artist made it, how unusual the lines are, how unique it is. Then we talk about imagination in drawing, writing, or play. They don't even bother to look the next time, because it has been explained logically. It's the same thing as if they were drawing a picture of a house. All houses are different, or we draw them different, because that is what our own eyes see.

I personally feel every child should know about birth control. It does not mean they have to use it, but we need to educate them in what "some" people use. We explain the consequences, that they are responsible for their bodies.

One method being used by teenagers today is douching. Douching IS NOT a method of birth control. If anything, it will cause the sperm to travel faster up the vaginal track. Douching with soda pop is not a method of birth control either.

If menstrual periods are not regular, it does not mean you can't get pregnant. What this means is that it will be harder to tell if you are pregnant. You can get pregnant while you are having your period. The chances are against it, but it has happened.

It does not matter what position you are in during sexual intercourse, pregnancy can occur. If you are breast feeding, you are less likely to become pregnant, but it can occur.

Those are all the methods which do not work for birth control. The following are methods that can work sometimes. I would also like to point out, as would every female in existence, that it is both the male's and the female's responsibility.

Classified as better than no birth control at all is withdrawl. We must remember that before ejaculation there are always some semen which are released. One drop of semen contains millions of sperm. If the penis is next to the vagina there is a chance of pregnancy occurring. The withdrawl method is a promise that the male makes to the female. He promises that he will pull his penis out before he ejaculates. This is, however, already too late. If the penis is in the vagina, there has already been a transfer of sperm.

The rhythm method of birth control is quite complicated. There are now ovulation kits on the market. An ovulation kit will tell you when you are ovulating, and this is when you refrain from sex. Many women also use it to tell them when they should have sex in order to get pregnant. The old fashioned rhythm method is to keep a chart of when you are ovulating. Ovulation occurs approximately 14–16 days after the first day of your period. There are some women who can tell by themselves when they are ovulating. There may be discomfort in the abdomen area, or where the ovaries are located. The texture of the mucus from the vagina will differ. There may be a slight discharge which is thicker in texture than normal, but it will be a clear discharge. A doctor from Australia claims if you put a drop of vaginal discharge in between two fingers, and separate the fingers, ovulation is occurring, if the mucus does not separate all the way. (Like a drop of water vs. something thicker in texture.) Many religions recommend the rhythm method. And actually, there are no drugs involved which may mix up your hormones. Perhaps if one were to check for ovulation for six months, and double check ovulation with a kit, it may be pretty reliable. If one would abstain from sex for three or four days on either side of ovulation, it would be better than no birth control at all. We must also remember that sperm can live in the vagina for two days.

Using a vaginal foam, jelly, or suppository which can be purchased in any drug store is not foolproof, although using this along with a condom does work very well. The foam has ingredients to kill sperm, and the condom is used to catch the sperm as it leaves the opening of the penis. One other plus of using a spermicide is it may help protect against a sexual disease. The condom will also help protect against this. A spermicide must always be inserted into the vagina a certain amount of time before having sex, so directions must be read very carefully. Always read directions for all birth control methods.

A condom is a very thin piece of rubber placed over the penis as soon as it is erect, and before it comes in contact with the vagina. The condom is said to have a 10–50 percent failure rate. This bears on both preventing pregnancy and sexually transmitted diseases. A condom should always be checked when taken out of the package. Always check by looking, to determine if there are any leaks. If the condom leaks, it will not work for protection. The condom, the second choice next to abstinence, is the next best thing to help guard against AIDS. Condoms can be purchased at any drug store. They come in all sorts of varieties, and are said not to decrease physical feeling during sex. A condom is used only once, and not to be shared. Care must be taken that condoms do not slip off prematurely.

The diaphragm is a thin piece of rubber in the shape of a little bowl that is to be placed over the opening of the woman's cervix. This will prevent sperm from entering the cervix. Every woman is different in the size of her cervix, and must be seen by a physician. The physician will measure the size of her cervix and will prescribe the right one for her. Along with the diaphragm, a spermicide must also be used. Both must be in place before sexual intercourse and be left in place for up to eight hours after sex. If the diaphragm and spermicide are used correctly, there is only a one in one hundred chance of pregnancy occurring.

An IUD sets up an environment that is hostile for egg implantation. The IUD is becoming less favorable to women because of the risk of infection in the uterus. An IUD is placed in the uterus by a physician, and is left there unless any problems occur. It is usually checked once a year. The chance of pregnancy with an IUD is approximately three out of one hundred. An IUD increases the chances of infection within the tubes, uterus, and ovaries.

The contraceptive sponge is relatively new on the market. The contraceptive sponge increases the risk of toxic shock syndrome, because it is left in the body. Leaving something that is foreign in our bodies always increases the risk of infection.

The birth control pill is almost a 100 percent effective way to protect against pregnancy. There are various strengths of the birth control pill, and your doctor will determine which is best for you. The "pill" makes the body think it is pregnant, and the ovaries cease to drop an egg every month. The hormone birth control pill must be taken on a daily basis depending upon what kind of pill you take. A pill cannot be missed for it is the series which make it effective. Your health history is very important to your doctor if they do prescribe the birth control pill. Always be very sure you tell them everything so that your particular history will not induce complications.

TO BE OR NOT TO BE . . . A VIRGIN

Virginity is an increasingly smart alternative to sexual relations, given the increased danger of diseases such as AIDS. Keeping to oneself may involve masturbation—but the risks of this activity are far less than thoughtlessly engaging in sex.

Our bodies belong to us, and WE are the ones who get to decide what is to be done with them. We have the power to say "Yes" and the power to say "No." Sexual activity among the young, and that means boys and girls, is starting at an earlier age every year. One third of all 16-year-old girls have had sexual intercourse. Forty-three percent of all 17-year-old girls have had sexual intercourse. By the time they reach 19 years, over 70 percent will have had intercourse. So, obviously, more are saying "Yes" than are saying "No."

The parent is really in no position to determine what is to be done with their child's body. It is ultimately up to the child. And just what is the right age to have sex? It really doesn't matter what age you are, what matters is if you fully realize what is at stake and are ready to face the consequences. Are you ready to have a baby? I'm not ready to have a baby. Mentally speaking, one should be about 60 before they have a child, but then, the body doesn't work like that. Do you know exactly what diseases you can catch, and are you willing to pay the price? What if you became sterile and could never have a baby . . . ever? And what if you died?

It doesn't work that way, does it? Do we ever think of those things when we're all hot and heavy? The unfortunate thing about it is, we should not get all hot and heavy anymore without all becoming doctors in our own right. We have to think before we even start kissing. We have to know the risks.

It doesn't matter if you're a virgin anymore, not in the sense that it used to. Being a virgin is the least of our worries at this time. We are not in the days of "free sex" any longer, it is the day, right now, when we may have to PAY for our sex—possibly with our life. This is not a laughing matter.

It is up to us whether or not we can pull ourselves out of this. Each one of us must be willing to sacrifice something. Each, and every, one of us. The sacrifices will vary. Some will sacrifice lives, while others will only sacrifice 10 cc's of blood for a test. The question is: For the first time in the history of this world, will we do it? I am, of course, talking about AIDS. Persons will have to sacrifice something, including pleasure, to prevent ignorant or accidental spreading of AIDS.

I want us first to relax. Sit down in your favorite chair, or better yet . . . pull your covers up around you and snuggle into your bed. Put the TV off, and turn off the radio. Make sure the door is closed. You are alone with your thoughts. It is nice to be alone. Practice putting pictures in your mind. Nice pictures, the things you like. You have no place to go right now. It doesn't matter what you don't have done . . . it will always keep. You can do it later.

Picture in your mind . . . your very best friend. It can be a lover . . . it can be your husband . . . it is the one you love. You see their face, the face that makes you like yourself. See their eyes looking at you. The creases in their face, around their mouth. They are smiling at you . . . they love you . . . too.

Our friends need us right now, and it doesn't even matter who they are. They are each one of us.

You have to see that face . . . of the one you love . . . to help us realize what we have done.

SEXUALLY TRANSMITTED DISEASES

It takes two to tango–but it takes three to spread a disease.

We have a problem. A problem that's spreading at an unbelievable rate. Sexually transmitted diseases. It's called AIDS, chlamydia, herpes, gonorrhea and syphilis. The diseases have only one good thing in common, and that is: HOW NOT TO GET THEM OR SPREAD THEM.

It is estimated that 10 MILLION to 12 MILLION Americans are infected with a sexually transmitted disease each year.

HOW NOT TO CATCH OR SPREAD A SEXUAL DISEASE

(1) The number one way not to catch a sexually transmitted disease is not to have sex.

(2) If you do have sex, know your partner. Knowing your partner means knowing for CERTAIN they are not having sex with anyone else. If your partner has sex with even ONE other person—there is a chance they might be carrying a disease and can give it to you.

(3) If you are not CERTAIN that you and your partner are FREE of every sexually transmitted disease–get tested before engaging in sex. Both of you.

(4) If you or your partner test positive for any sexually transmitted disease–it is your responsibility as a caring human being to notify every person you have had sex with.

(5) If you and your partner are both free of disease–LIMIT SEX TO THAT ONE PARTNER.

So, what's the next step? Even if you follow the rules, there's another precaution you can take. Use a condom. The condom can be purchased at any drug store, it is relatively cheap, and there are no side effects. I repeat: a condom can be used only once and it is not to be shared. It should also be checked, even if it's right out of the package, for any leaks. Use it–it may mean your life.

If you have questions on sexually transmitted diseases or would like to be tested, and are afraid to talk with your family doctor, there are others whom you can talk to. The public health department in your state can refer you to the clinic nearest you. Or you can look in the yellow pages under clinics or social service organizations. If you don't call the correct number the first try, don't give up, try again. Remember, they don't have to know who you are when you're calling just for information. For example: "Hi . . . I live in the city of _____, and I would like some information on herpes (or whatever). (Or: I would like to be tested for _____). Could you please give me the phone number of clinics in my area?" If finding a phone number in the white or yellow pages seems too confusing, you can always call your local information number or the operator. And also, your local public safety department is there to serve you and can give you the numbers to call.

If, at any time, one has a test for gonorrhea, AIDS or syphillis, and it turns out to be positive—the doctor is obligated to report the results to the state health department and in the case of gonorrhea or syphilis any sexual contacts you may have had.

This may not be the case, however, with chlamydia and herpes. It is always difficult to confront a problem such as this—to tell someone you may have passed something on to them. So we will acknowledge the fact some people are too afraid to tell the other person. What can you do? There is always the possibility of informing someone anonymously—at least they will know the truth and can get treated. You would never want someone to go on with a disease maybe to become sterile for life, or die, right? Hopefully, they will not give it to anybody else.

The professional who gives you the positive results more than likely will ask you if you know who you had contact with and if you will tell them. Your automatic response will be, "Yes. Of course I know, and I will tell them."

But what if time goes by and you still haven't told them? They may have given it to another person who in turn will give it to two others. That's at least three more people who have it now. This is how it spreads. And it happens so quickly.

If you are afraid to tell that person, talk to someone you trust. Your high school counselor, an adult friend, a crisis center, the public safety juvenile department, a teacher you trust. What would be best, however, is confronting the problem right when you hear the words, "Your test is positive." Talk to that professional. They already know the results. No surprises there. Ask them questions if you have any. Or call them back with questions. They know the difficulty that lies ahead. They will have the resources at hand to help you right then and there.

AIDS—THE KILLER

AIDS is no longer a killer disease associated only with homosexuals, bisexuals, prostitutes, drug addicts or foreigners. It is now killing healthy heterosexuals who may live in our own neighborhood. That means it can kill you, me, your mom, or your dad.

Unlike other sexually transmitted diseases such as chlamydia, gonorrhea, and syphilis—AIDS has no cure. There is no vaccine available to guard against getting it, and it cannot be cured by a simple injection or pill.

By the year 1991, AIDS will have killed more Americans than both the Vietnam and Korean wars combined. And it is believed that this particular projection is conservative. At the end of 1986, more than 29,000 Americans contracted AIDS. By the year 1991, according to most estimates, 270,000 people will contract AIDS; 179,000 will die—and new cases involving heterosexuals will probably multiply by 10, bringing the number of heterosexuals infected with AIDS to 23,000. Also by the year 1991, 4,000 babies will have gotten AIDS from their mothers. The Center for Disease Control states that 1.5 MILLION Americans NOW carry the AIDS virus but do not indicate symptoms. They do not know they are carriers. Other experts are estimating this number is actually 4 MILLION.

Dr. June Osborn, dean of the School of Public Health at the University of Michigan said, "People have to understand that getting AIDS has nothing to do with whether you're black, homosexual or Haitian. It's not who you are but WHAT YOU DO."

Ten million people in the world now carry the AIDS virus. Ninety-one nations have reported AIDS cases. Homosexual AIDS cases now account for two-thirds of the reported cases. One in four new AIDS cases can be connected to drug addicts. AIDS has the potential to wipe out an entire population. It's not just the gay American's disease any longer. IT IS OUR DISEASE.

You cannot get AIDS by shaking hands with someone who has AIDS or is an AIDS carrier. However, if you have sex with someone who has AIDS, ARC (AIDS Related Complex), or is an AIDS carrier—You can get AIDS. If you use drugs that are injected and use a needle someone else has used—who has AIDS, ARC, or is an AIDS carrier—YOU CAN GET AIDS.

Having anal sex has the highest risk potential in spreading AIDS. Vaginal sex ranks second and oral sex, third. It is not known at this time whether AIDS can be spread by wet (French) kissing.

There is no known cure for AIDS. The AIDS (Acquired Immune Deficiency Syndrome) virus has the potential to destroy all white blood cells in the body. White blood cells are what protect us against infections and diseases. If we don't have these white blood cells to protect us, it leaves us open to minor infections that can, in turn, develop into life-threatening infections or cancers.

Most AIDS victims do not live for more than two or three years once the symptoms of AIDS develop. And it is now known people can harbor the AIDS virus for at least 10 years without showing symptoms. Or, as one doctor put it, "It can go back sixty years . . . we just don't know." What we do know for sure, however, is that NO ONE IS IMMUNE FROM AIDS.

At this point, March 1987, the officials are reporting: You cannot get AIDS from shaking hands or by coming in contact with the sweat of an AIDS carrier. The AIDS virus has not yet been identified in sweat or perspiration. AIDS has been identified in very small amounts in tears and saliva. However, health officials at this time do not think you can get AIDS by sharing a drinking glass with an AIDS victim or coming in contact with the tears of an AIDS victim.

They say at this point in time, March 1987: You cannot get AIDS from social kissing, coughing, sneezing, eating food fixed by someone with AIDS, insect bites or ear piercing.

How can you find out if you have AIDS or have been exposed to the AIDS virus? By a blood test that is done in a clinic or doctor's office. All states have clinics designated to offer free and confidential testing. Your state health department will be able to refer you to the clinic nearest you. The results of the test usually take two to three weeks.

The following are the warning signs or symptoms of AIDS. It must be taken into consideration, however, that many of the symptoms may be symptoms of something other than AIDS. It is also important to note the symptoms of AIDS are ALWAYS . . . PERSISTENT, UNEXPLAINED, AND RECURRENT. If these symptoms present themselves to you or someone you know, you should contact a physician or clinic immediately, and please, PLEASE, refrain from any sexual contact until the cause is determined. It may mean more than one life.

- rapid weight loss, meaning 20 pounds or more within two weeks
- night sweats or fever
- dry, unproductive cough
- profound, unexplained fatigue
- swollen glands or lymph nodes under the armpits, groin area, or neck
- severe diarrhea lasting more than one week

- white spots or unusual blemishes in the mouth or throat area
- shortness of breath not associated with allergies or cigarette smoking
- recent appearance of pink or purple blotches on or under the skin

If one tests positive for AIDS—what does this mean? If you or someone you know tests positive for AIDS, it means you or they have tested positive for the ANTIBODY for AIDS; it means you or they have tested positive for the ANTIBODY to the AIDS virus. There has been an exposure to the AIDS virus. If one tests positive for AIDS, it doesn't necessarily mean you or they have the AIDS virus, have ARC (AIDS Related Complex), have the symptoms of AIDS or have AIDS itself. There has been an exposure to AIDS (the VIRUS of AIDS) and the blood indicates the antibody.

It is not the AIDS virus, itself, that can kill you, but rather, what the virus can do to your body. Deadly infections or cancers cannot be fought off, because the AIDS virus destroys the body's immune system. If someone who has AIDS gets a cold, the cold could quickly develop into pneumonia and be life-threatening.

The U.S. Public Health Service has now estimated that probably 20 percent of all the people who harbor the AIDS virus in their bodies will go on to develop AIDS within five years. It is not known at this time how long it may take an individual who carries the AIDS virus to develop AIDS. It has been estimated, however, at least 50 percent of the people who have the AIDS virus will eventually develop AIDS.

Once a person has the AIDS virus in his system, there are some precautions he or she can take. The precautions are hardly reassuring. It is suggested: to avoid contact with other infections, get enough rest, eat nutritional foods, and avoid exposure to other venereal diseases. The only way to guard against AIDS is to guard against getting the virus in the first place.

Research on AIDS is in a frantic state. Scientists are faced with a miniscule element that can be likened to that of an atomic nucleus in its potential to destroy. If one has the AIDS virus, even if no symptoms are present, that person will have the virus for life. It would be like living on an earthquake fault-line, and having CONCRETE evidence in your hand, there will BE an earthquake—SOON.

Only, you can't run for cover, or escape the consequences. Others will try to help you, and they will try to help you, but they will be unable to help you. They can only try to make you as comfortable as possible until it is time for you to face your death. And you will suffer while you wait.

At this time, there is only one drug available to help AIDS patients. It is called AZT. AZT is not a cure, but it is a major advance. The drug can extend the lives of some AIDS patients, although it is not yet clear as for how long. AZT has serious side effects, one being anemia. However, the benefits are enough to indicate at least the AIDS virus is penetrable. This opens other avenues to be explored for other drugs and treatments.

At this time, AIDS patients all over the world are trying experimental drugs. However, the National Academy of Sciences recently reported: Neither vaccines or satisfactory drug therapies for AIDS are likely to be available in the near future.

Where do we go from here, people? Where, indeed. I recently asked my doctor if he thought I should have a test for AIDS. He was taken back. "What?" he replied.

"But shouldn't everybody be tested for AIDS?" I asked.

"Well, we could test you if you wanted, but you're married," he said.

"But I was married once before . . . how can I know?" I replied. "And, I had sex before I was married the second time," I admitted.

"But what if the test came out positive," he stated grimly.

There was silence on both ends of the phone and then he added, "The AIDS virus can be in the body for at least ten years before it surfaces."

I thought quietly on that one. I had been married for eight years. I had remained monogamous. Had my huband remained monogamous? I was pretty sure he had . . . but how do you ever know, for sure? I knew my sexual history, and even if there had only been two other people before, that meant how many others THOSE two people had been with sexually? If I didn't know . . . how on earth could I know my husband's end of it?

"Are you there?" he asked.

"Yes, I'm right here," I answered.

"So, if you had the test and it turned out to be positive, what would you do?" he asked.

"I don't really know WHAT I would do . . . but at least I would KNOW . . . wouldn't I?"

AIDS is out there. We cannot turn back the clock. And we can't wish it away. All we can do is wait until someone comes up with a remedy. In the meantime, hundreds of thousands of us will die from it. At this time, I believe the only answer we have a chance with is if we do know, individually – if we have it or not. If you or me are carriers. And then to STAY SAFE.

New findings in the research in AIDS is happening daily. One day I had asked if AIDS could be found in cats and dogs. What if they were immune? What if they were carriers? The next day a French research report came out stating cats carried a virus similar to AIDS but as a different strain. The findings in AIDS will now move very quickly—to keep up you must read your daily newspaper or contact the various health agencies. Some of the medical details I have cited about AIDS may be seen as primitive, or even wrong, as research continues. But the precautions against catching AIDS are and will continue to be correct.

I am going to repeat the ways on how to prevent catching or spreading a sexual disease . . . this is how important it is. It is up to each one of us as to what happens from here on in.

- The number one way not to catch a sexually transmitted disease is not to have sex anally, vaginally, or orally.
- If you do decide to have sex, know your partner. Knowing your partner means knowing for certain they are not having sex with anyone else. If your partner has sex with even one other person—you cannot be certain you will not get a disease. If your partner's one other person does have a sexual disease, your partner will give it to you.
- If you are not certain you and your partner are FREE of every sexually transmitted disease—GET TESTED before engaging in sex. Both of you.
- If you or your partner test positive for any sexually transmitted disease—it is the responsibility of both of you to notify every person you have had sex with.
- If you and your partner are both free of disease—LIMIT SEX TO YOUR PARTNER—NO EXCEPTIONS!
- Use a condom just to be safe.

My own, personal, opinion on all of this? Who needs a nuclear war when we have this? AIDS has the potential to wipe us all out. We have all our research up to this point, on how we can catch it or how we can't . . . I don't buy it. There have been too many times in history when something has been overlooked. We're only human. We make mistakes. Who, in their right mind, has the right to say for sure? We have to take precautions and we have to sacrifice—if only an hour of our time to have a blood sample taken.

And then we have everybody afraid of what it may mean to this country, the United States, if we were to have mandatory testing. It's against our constitution. Who says it is fair that a minority dictates to us, if we should live or die? We have a major issue here. It is unique to each country, and each country must decide how it is going to get rid of the enemy, the virus.

And, this is not big brother, it is being the brother to our fellow man. This . . . is bigger than anything we have ever had to face as a nation. And yes, our freedom IS at stake, we have to take care of the problem now, before our freedom of living is lost.

Adolescents, you are left in a very difficult position. The parents of my generation apologized for putting us in that time-frame, they were sorry we had to face drugs and a senseless war. You, I am afraid, have to face a lot more. And more than ever, we have to take the time to help you deal with it. We need to spend the time to teach you.

If you would like to know more about AIDS or would like more current, updated information, here is where you will find it:

Telephone Hotlines (Toll Free)
PHS AIDS Hotline 1-800-342-AIDS
1-800-342-2437

National Sexually Transmitted Diseases Hotline/American Social Health Association 1-800-227-8922

National Gay Task Force
AIDS Information Hotline 1-800-221-7044 or (212) 807-6016 (NY State)

Information Sources
U.S. Public Health Service Public Affairs Office; Hubert H. Humphrey Building, Room 725-H, 200 Independence Avenue, S.W., Washington, D.C. 20201, Phone: (202) 245-6867

Local Red Cross or American Red Cross AIDS Education Office, 1730 D Street, N.W., Washington, D.C. 20006, Phone: (202) 737-8300

Other
American Association of Physicians for Human Rights, P.O. Box 14366, San Francisco, CA 94114, Phone: (415) 558-9353

AIDS Action Council, 729 Eighth Street, S.E., Suite 200, Washington, D.C. 20003, Phone: (202) 547-3101

Gay Men's Health Crisis, P.O. Box 274, 132 West 24th Street, New York, NY 10011, Phone: (212) 807-6655

Hispanic AIDS Forum c/o APRED, 853 Broadway, Suite 2007, New York, NY 10003, Phone: (212) 870-1902 or 870-1864

Los Angeles AIDS Project, 1362 Santa Monica Boulevard, Los Angeles, CA 90046, Phone: (213) 871-AIDS

Minority Task Force on AIDS, c/o New York City Council of Churches, 475 Riverside Drive, Room 456, New York, NY 10115, Phone: (212) 749-1214

Mothers of AIDS Patients, (MAP), c/o Barbara Peabody, 3403 E. Street, San Diego, CA 92102, Phone: (619) 234-3432

National AIDS Network, 729 Eighth Street, S.E., Suite 300, Washington, D.C. 20003, Phone: (202) 546-2424

National Association of People with AIDS, P.O. Box 65472, Washington, D.C. 20035, Phone: (202) 483-7979

National Coalition of Gay Sexually Transmitted Disease Services, c/o Mark Behar, P.O. Box 239, Milwaukee, WI 53201, Phone: (414) 277-7671

National Council of Churches/AIDS Task Force, 475 Riverside Drive, Room 572, New York, NY 10115, Phone: (212) 870-2421

San Francisco AIDS Foundation, 333 Valencia Street, 4th Floor, San Francisco, CA 94103, Phone: (415) 863-2437

From InterAmerica Research

Surgeon General's Report on AIDS: Free from InterAmerica Research, 1200 E. North Henry Street, Alexandria,VA 22314. Free pamphlets:
"Gay and Bisexual Men and AIDS."
"Caring for the AIDS Patient at Home and If Your Test for Antibody to the AIDS Virus Is Positive."
"Facts About AIDS and Drug Abuse."
"AIDS and Children."
"AIDS and Children: Information for Teachers and School Officials."
"AIDS and Your Job—Are There Risks?"
"Coping with AIDS."

From the Office of Public Inquiries

Office of Public Inquiries, Centers for Disease Control, Building 1, Room B-63, 1600 Clifton Road, Atlanta, GA 30333. Free booklets:
"What Gay and Bisexual Men Should Know About AIDS."
"AIDS and Shooting Drugs."
"Why You Should Be Informed About AIDS."

Other

Free: Answers About AIDS, send a self-addressed business-size envelope with 66 cents postage attached, mail to AIDS Report, American Council on Science and Health, 47 Maple Street, Summit, NJ 07901.

CHLAMYDIA

Chlamydia is the most widespread sexually transmitted disease of today. The symptoms are often very mild and may resemble symptoms of gonorrhea. And often, people who have chlamydia don't know they have it.

Chlamydia trachomatis is a bacterium named for the Greek word "chlamys," meaning cloak. And until recently, it has mainly been associated with trachoma, an eye disease found mainly in underdeveloped countries. It is estimated over 500 MILLION people in the world have trachoma, with blindness occurring in approximately 2 million of the cases.

When chlamydia is transmitted sexually, a variety of medical problems can occur. In males, it is the leading cause of nongonococcal urethritis, or NGU, which is an inflammation of the urethra. It may resemble the main symptom of gonorrhea. Cases of chlamydia in the U.S. male are now double that of gonorrhea. When left untreated, it can result in epididymitis, inflammation of the testicles. It can go on to cause sterility. Every year, over 250,000 of the 500,000 cases of epididymitis are caused by chlamydia. Other complications may include protitis (anal inflammation in homosexuals) and Reiter's syndrome, an arthritis-like condition.

The consequences of chlamydia in women are even more severe than in that of the male. It usually begins as a cervix infection. If this is untreated it may spread through the uterus and on into the fallopian tubes. The fallopian tubes can be blocked by scar tissue, which in turn, can cause infertility or an ectopic pregnancy. An ectopic pregnancy is when fertilized egg begins development outside the uterus. Ectopic pregnancies can be life-threatening.

Chlamydia can also cause lymphogranuloma venereum and psittacosis pneumonia (or "parrot-fever"). Chlamydia can cause pelvic inflammatory disease, or PID. PID is the inflammation of the female reproductive organs. Each year in the U.S. more than 1 million women are treated for PID. Over 200,000 are hospitalized. In pregnant women, chlamydia can spread to the baby during childbirth. It can cause a spontaneous miscarriage or stillbirth. It can also cause fatal infections in new mothers after birth.

It is now estimated over 3 million people in the U.S. suffer seriously from chlamydia. This is not taking into account the cases which go unreported. And, in 60–80 percent of female cases and in 10 percent of the male cases, THERE ARE NO SYMPTOMS.

Observable symptoms include: (Male) painful urination and watery discharge from the penis. (Female) itching or burning sensation in the genital area, vaginal discharge, dull pelvic pain and bleeding in between menstrual periods.

Unfortunately, testing for chlamydia is not usually done routinely during a check-up. The patient will probably have to be the one to ask for the test. There are two species of chlamydia: one responds to antibiotic drugs and the other does not. Tests can be done either by blood or a culture. Results may take from one to three days.

Researchers are working on developing a vaccine against chlamydia; however, in the meantime–know your sex partner and use a condom and diaphragm to help protect against it. If any of the symptoms do occur, contact your physician or clinic immediately and don't forget to tell your partner if you have it. They will need treatment too.

HERPES

There are over 50 varieties of herpes, and within the realm of all these viruses, they affect over 75 million Americans, perhaps even up to 150 million, including chicken pox and mononucleosis. Of the genital herpes, statistics indicate that they affect over 20 million Americans, and that there are over 500,000 new cases each year.

Within the realm of herpes, it continues (as it seems many of our topics do) to be a very controversial issue. The strain of herpes we will concern ourselves with is that of the herpes simplex genitalis, known as Herpes II. However, in speaking with many experts on the subject, many of them felt that the herpes which shows up as a cold sore or fever blister, Herpes I, actually is the same as Herpes II in the genital area . . . both being contracted in different areas. But being there IS a small molecular difference in the herpes virus cell. Thus, it DOES actually make a difference.

In looking into the subject, I had no idea of what lay before me. What a mess! In talking with a scientist who is actually working on a vaccine to immunize persons who have never had herpes . . . against ever getting it, I got even more confused. This doctor felt herpes actually has been around since the beginning of time, and that you can find strains of herpes virus within plants and most animals. Apparently pigs are having a big bout with it, too. So, how in the world do you not come in contact with herpes? For such an old subject, herpes has only been actively researched for about 15 years. Therefore, many questions exist and will remain for the time being.

How do you actually get herpes? From skin to skin contact or mucous membrane to mucous membrane. Herpes is a virus which enters the cells and causes a blistering infection which then travels up into the spine and stays there in a dormant state reactivating from time to time. In genital herpes, symptoms occur after a couple of days to three weeks after exposure. The first symptom may be burning, itching, or numbness, with headaches, fever, and muscle aches. (Like the flu.) After around 10 days a cluster of bumps may form, causing blisters and then an ulcer. This or these ulcers can be very painful, and may last for weeks. In talking with the Herpes Resource Center, they reported that there is now a drug available for persons who are getting herpes. This is not a cure, however. What it does is shorten the time period you are afflicted with the initial attack or outbreak. Persons who already have herpes cannot use this. This drug is called Zovirax, and it helps the immune system to fight off the virus. It is by prescription only. There has been progress in controlling attacks of genital herpes. One especially valuable medicine is Acyclovir.

One of the most frequently asked questions is: can you get herpes off a toilet seat? Chances are 99.9% against it. One study was done by using a viral fluid which was left on a toilet seat. After two hours the virus still remained. However, this would have to mean someone with herpes would have had to have deposited enough viral fluid onto the toilet seat, and if it were a woman to come in contact with it, she would have to straddle the toilet seat. But then again, it is not yet known if herpes can travel from skin through skin, with the skin being a dry surface (basically) and the virus drifting through, so to speak.

Once a person does have an initial attack of herpes, the virus travels up through the spine and lies dormant until reactivated. Experts are not quite sure just exactly how or why the virus gets reactivated, but they think stress is a factor, or lack of sleep, poor diet or friction from tight jeans. It is also recommended that chocolate, nuts and coffee be avoided.

Some people have reoccurrences of herpes every couple of months, and some never experience it again. If a woman is pregnant and has a reoccurrence of the symptoms a week or two before birth, chances are the baby will contract the virus, and statistics do indicate 65 percent of those babies will die or have brain damage. Therefore, the woman should be tested a few weeks before the birth and a c-section administered if the virus is present at that time.

The best possible way to avoid herpes is not to kiss, have skin or sexual contact with anyone who shows any of the symptoms. If one has a lip blister and then has oral genital contact, it WILL be transferred. It is also believed that use of a condom will reduce the risk of contacting herpes. However, in the testing process, human beings were not used, and they don't know if actual intercourse would affect the condom in such a way that the virus could get through anyway. During an outbreak it is also best to keep the infected area clean and dry.

Some researchers feel that there is an increased risk of cervical cancer for women who have herpes. However, the risk is believed to be slight and is not entirely founded.

If there is a suspicion of herpes it should always be diagnosed by a doctor . . . never diagnosed by yourself. There are always other things it could be.

So . . . what to do regarding this panoramic problem? Probably the biggest issue to tackle is . . . not to panic. A normal life is possible, and you are the one to run your life . . . not a herpes virus. If you do have herpes, the more you worry about it, the more often it is likely to reoccur.

Having herpes does not mean you are a leper or have cancer. It is a terrible inconvenience at times, and it is something which requires responsible precautions. It does not mean you cannot have sex ever again, but rather to evaluate any symptoms you may have BEFORE having sex. It is recommended that you abstain from sex 72 hours after the lesions have disappeared.

Many people find relief by joining a self-help group with other persons who also have herpes. Any public health department can steer you in the correct direction. Once you have contracted herpes, the initial attack is usually the worst and every reoccurrence will lessen with time. Women who have herpes should always have a yearly pap smear, if only to keep tabs on the situation.

It appears that some people can be immune to herpes, although this continues to be inconclusive. There are cases where one party does have herpes and the second party never shows any signs or symptoms. It is estimated that 75–90 percent of the population does have some form of herpes virus, so if you are sexually active with one or more persons, quite honestly, it probably is highly likely that you will come in contact with it in one form or another.

All you can really do is to take as many precautions as you can, know your sex partner, and try to turn on the light to check out the situation yourself. Although, in women a lesion can be well hidden within the vagina.

Referrals: Herpes Resource Center (formerly HELP), a program service of the American Social Health Association, P.O. Box 100, Palo Alto, Calif. 94302 (800-227-8922); and the Venereal Disease Control Division of the Centers for Disease Control, Atlanta, GA 30333 (404-329-3311).

GONORRHEA

If you are sexually active, there is a very good chance you may get gonorrhea. It is estimated that over two million cases were contracted in the United States during 1981, and that adds up to a new contact for gonorrhea every 15 seconds. One case of gonorrhea is reported every two minutes, and in the United States it will affect 1 out of 20 people. Three out of four of these cases will occur in people ages 15–19.

Gonorrhea is contracted by sexual contact. However, a wet finger touching a moist surface will also spread the disease. Gonorrhea is more easily noticed in the male, and shows up as a discharge or burning sensation. Gonorrhea can also be contracted through the rectum or mouth. If in the mouth, it could mean a redness or swelling of the throat. However, if in the vagina, usually there are no symptoms at all. If gonorrhea goes untreated, it can cause severe pain in the reproductive organs, eventually sterility, arthritis, heart disease or blindness.

The only way you can tell if you have gonorrhea is through a simple lab culture. If there has been sexual contact other than with the penis and vagina, such as the mouth or rectum, an additional culture must be taken.

There are a few ways to help prevent contact with gonorrhea. Of course, number one is no sexual contact. Number two is to know your sex partner. There should be enough respect and caring involved to tell the other if you suspect anything. Washing the genital area after intercourse with soap and water helps. Urinating helps flush it out. And one other good way is to use a condom.

If there is reason to believe you may have contacted gonorrhea, there are many clinics and doctors available to help you, and in most states you do not need your parents' permission.

Gonorrhea is treated by a dose of penicillin given by injection, and it is recommended that if you are sexually active with more than one person, you should have a culture taken every three months. If there is only one person, a yearly check should be done.

SYPHILIS

"Syphilis is the third most frequently reported communicable disease in the United States. In 1980, 27,515 cases of primary and secondary syphilis were reported, representing an increase of 10 percent over 1979. The number of unreported cases has been estimated to be two or three times greater.

"The reported incidence of syphilis appears higher in nonwhites than in whites and in urban than in rural areas. These differences partly reflect the fact that indigent urban racial groups are treated in public clinics where case reporting is complete.

"Syphilis is most common in the sexually active years peaking between 20 and 24 years of age, with a range of most new cases occurring between 15 and 40 years of age. The male–female ratio of early cases is about 2 to 1 in the U.S."[7]

Syphilis is contracted most commonly by sexual contact, although there have been cases where it has been spread by kissing. After 10–90 days after being infected, a small sore called a chancre will most likely appear. Or it may be a large relatively painless sore likened to that of a pimple and be open and runny. This is the first stage of syphilis. The sore normally appears where the contact has been made, usually the genital area. However, it may surface in other areas such as on a finger, breast, anus, mouth, or lips. If a female has contracted syphilis, it may go unnoticed and undetected if it is inside the vagina.

The secondary signs of syphilis may be a light rash covering any part of the body, fever, headache, sore throat, sores, or hair falling out. During both the primary stages and by the secondary stage of syphilis, it is highly contagious and can be readily spread by sexual contact.

If syphilis goes untreated, there may be heart disease, blindness, paralysis, deformity, or insanity. In the latent stages of syphilis, 20 years can pass before these other symptoms make themselves known.

The best way to not get syphilis is to, of course, not have sexual contact. Once a partner has syphilis, he can give it to his partner anytime, anywhere along the way. Again, know you sex partner and don't be afraid to check them out in the bright light.

To test for syphilis a blood sample is taken, and it is treated by an injection of penicillin.

It appears to me that many of the symptoms of herpes may resemble some of the symptoms of syphilis, so I would suggest that if ANY symptom appears, it would be wise to have it checked out with a clinic or a doctor. Only a professional and a simple lab test can confirm the real cause of the symptoms.

Really . . . the only way to put a stop to these epidemics is to take precautions and be responsible for your actions. And if you think you may have symptoms . . . check them out . . . and TELL the person you

---

[7] Reprinted from *The Management of Infectious Diseases in Clinical Practice*, Edited by Phillip K. Peterson, M.D., L. D. Sabath, M.D., Ernesto Caldero'n J., M.D., and Allan R. Ronald, M.D.: "SYPHILIS," by Jacques E. Mokhbat, Department of Medicine, University of Minnesota, Minneapolis, Minnesota, p. 45, ©1982 by Academic Press, Inc. Used by permission.

were with. It may be embarrassing and it may change the relationship, however, IT HAS TO BE DONE.

SUMMARY

To be . . . or not to be. A virgin. Actually, it's rather interesting. Instead of saving ourselves for our lifetime mate, we must save ourselves for "ourselves." We must be very selfish with whom we share ourselves sexually.

The temptation to feel "good" for a short amount of time must be outweighed with the knowledge of what can happen to us if we succumb. The question of sex being morally wrong is not the problem anymore. The diseases which can be spread sexually can kill us, they can make us sterile, and they can create many medical complications that can also kill us. We have to know that. And morality will, no doubt, follow behind without our even knowing it.

I just got off the phone with a mother of a twelve-year-old girl. The twelve-year-old girl's friends are going all the way. They are having sexual intercourse. They carry condoms with them. And my little friend, the twelve-year-old, is telling her friends what can happen to them. She is warning them of the dangers. This, is how it has to be. Every single one of our children must realize what is at stake. THEY MUST BE ABLE TO WARN EACH OTHER. And they will not be able to warn each other if they do not have the facts. We must educate them, we must set limits, and we must love them. They have to love themselves. It has to do with that little light shining within that makes us so important. We must be able to believe in ourselves and trust ourselves. We have to be able to say, "No," because WE don't want to, not because someone else wants us to. And remember, it doesn't matter what anyone else thinks of us, what matters is what we think of ourselves.

CHAPTER EIGHT

Our Time Has Come

*R*ESPONSIBILITIES. *WE ALL* have them, but what are they or what do they mean to the adolescent and the young adult? Responsibilities represent uncertainty. Uncertainties within the realm of others, other's actions, and ourselves and our own reactions.

Responsibilities mean finding our place in the world and taking chances. Taking risks we may sometimes not wish to take. Things do not come easy in this world, and dues must be paid in one form or another. Let us get that straight right off the bat . . . nothing is EVER for free. We do not get a free ride, and sometimes we may have to pay two or three times before we can hop on the trolley just to go a block or two.

Within every goal we strive to attain lies accompanying pain. It may mean hard work, a lot of sweat . . . or perhaps a broken heart or two or three. But we survive because we have to. It's in our nature.

Ah . . . the sweet mystery of life. I don't think we EVER find its secret hidden amongst the nooks and crannies of the world.

> *Sweet mystery of life*
> *What will you bring to me*
>   *on this so quiet night.*
>
> *Soft lovers*
>   *who kiss with candlelight . . .*
> *Or maybe a moment*
>   *of sadness and strife.*
>
> *Oh, bring me a companion*
>   *to share this life*
> *One who understands . . .*
> *One who has seen the light.*

Sweet mystery of life
You placed a love in my heart
A peace in my soul.
Oh, bring me back to the land
    where we all belong
Among reality
    and the feeling of right.

Sweet mystery of life
I shall follow along your path
I will go where you lead
Follow the winds
    soft sound.
Around the bend.
Across calm waters bound.
You brought me to this place in time
    this moment of now.

I shall follow and listen
    to this new song
Find the answer
    to this sweet mystery
    of life.

(17 years old)

One of the most important aspects in life is for us to find a companion to share life with us. Some may not need it . . . but most do. And it's not easy finding someone who will share the joys with the sorrows, the good with the bad . . . at the same time. A heart can be broken many times, and although it may never heal completely, it survives, and gets stronger through the process.

Goodbye becomes one of the hardest words in the dictionary to utter. But it will be said, nonetheless in many places, in many ways, and through different avenues.

Leave me with long remembered moments
Of your hand touching mine.
Of never ending walks which could never catch the time.
Restless waves along the shore.
Never again . . .
Never more.

See the grey distant shadows of ships lost to sea,
And questioning, glancing looks
That seem to ask . . .
Should we?

Sailboats drift shyly through the sunset,
Fleeting moments . . . gone
Never to be met.

All I ask is for no more goodbyes
Give me no more farewells
No more whispers . . .
That time will only tell.

All I can see are disregarded flowers
Unfamiliar smiles . . .
With low, longing looks that last all the while.

Time has caught me by surprise
It is time and I must go,
Back to the land of ice and snow.
Where sorrows will be better kept
And fears and tears will not be wept.

Fly pretty bird . . . out to the sea.
Never, never look back,
That is the key.

Spread your wide, wide wings that will carry me
Back to my home
Where smiles are safe and so much better known.
Wise, wise bird . . . you'll set us free
Where you can be you
And I can be me.

You leave me with long remembered moments
Of your hand touching mine . . .
Of never ending walks which could never catch the time.
Restless waves along the shore
Never again . . .
Never more.

(21 years old)

GOAL SETTING

Goal setting and achieving are a couple of the most important aspects in life we can possibly teach our children. But how in the world do we go about teaching them how to set and achieve goals? Is success something which is inbred, or can we learn it? I believe it is a combination of the two.

In regard to my daughter, Jessica, I have done so much studying, reading, and experimenting, it's frightening. You see, in my heart I want her to succeed in what she is capable of or wants out of life. I guess I became so aware of what we are able to achieve in being aware of her first year of life. And it all revolves around correct and proper stimulation.

As Jessica lay in her isolette day after day, month after month, I watched the process of stimulation transpiring right before my very eyes in what the hospital staff portrayed. Even though she was only two pounds, she had a series of exercises she had to go through. Not strenuous mind you, but very subtle. Eye movement, touch, and physical activity. Sometimes it may have been changing the blanket she was lying on to a rougher texture or lying her on a different side, or changing her surroundings. It may seem ridiculous in trying to stimulate a two-pound baby, but believe me, it is not.

We, as human beings, use 10 percent of our brain power. I always thought this was something some scientist made up to make us think we were really stupid until I saw it proven to me. There was a study done in England of three children, all who were born with hydrocephalus (fluid in the brain). Ninety percent of their brains has been filled with fluid leaving them functioning with only the remaining 10 percent. What occurred was all three children, now adolescents and adults, were functioning normally. Better than normally. One of the adolescents is a genius in mathematics, one held two degrees and is a professor, and the other is also classified in the genius range.

When tests were taken of their brains, the two who had not been suctioned out at birth (removing the fluid) were left with the 10 percent of their brain slimly lined around the edges. Their mind activity was measured, and they learned they were operating only on that 10 percent. However, this ten percent was red hot and actually white with activity. Their activity centers within the brain had actually shifted to carry on responsibilities or tasks they previously, "supposedly" were not able to handle. So where is the answer? It has to be in stimulation.

Within the realm of intelligence, some believe it to be inherited and some believe it to be environmental. I believe it to be both. Many experts say that the intelligence of a child is determined by the average of both parents. However, if you take the original average and then add a stimulating environment . . . what do you get? You have an addition on to the original. However, it always depends on what you do with it. I believe it can be raised an additional 10 to 20 points.

If a young child is stimulated and is doing above average within his age group and is then placed with children who are functioning on an average level, that child will stay at his level . . . for the time being. What he will then do is wait for the others to catch up to him and then join them. Therefore, becoming the norm.

This is all very interesting, but you ask, what does this have to do with goal setting and achieving? Too many times we see our children performing at the norm, and we are happy and contented they are normal and average. What we don't realize is that we can place them in an even more stimulating environment, thus, increasing their potential of what we perceive them to be capable of. Yes, it is hard work, because we are the ones who have to work harder, and we may even have to do a little learning ourselves. It is not easy; however, in the process we will have stimulated ourselves along with our children, thereby, growing.

Basically, we never meet our goals, because we are taught not to. With every goal there are steps which have to be followed through in order to learn how to achieve larger goals. We must begin with small goals, and these small goals are EMINENTLY important, because we may not achieve them thinking they are too small to be bothered with.

After Jessica's birth, something happened to me. I lost track of myself for a while. In trying to regain or recapture myself, I talked with a psychologist. I found I was not meeting ANY goals, just drifting along and stagnating. My task was to make daily goals that were for me and only me, but what I liked to do. One was to relax in a hot tub after a long, hard day, one was to write a little, and other was to play the piano for five minutes out of the day. In the beginning I couldn't DO it. Really! I found other things needed to be done, and I couldn't find the time. I was finally convinced to give it a try. And it was hard, but I did them. I was happier, and my goals began to become larger with practice. I found you have to MAKE them happen.

Many times we as parents expect too much or too little of our children. When they fail at the smaller goals we don't even think they are capable of obtaining larger ones. Or we get frustrated and disgusted, because suddenly out of the blue we expect them to be able to obtain larger goals. And here we have the child ALSO feeling frustrated, because he doesn't and cannot achieve them. This is because he doesn't know HOW.

They need the guidance and assurance that they can achieve what they want to. Sure, they may always learn later in life . . . sometimes . . . how to achieve their goals. But believe me, it is a lot easier, satisfying, and you can achieve even more if you learn earlier.

Adolescents and young adults should have three goals. One goal should be a goal met every single day. Not a big one, but a small and satisfying one. Maybe it could be to read one chapter in a book they like on a daily basis. Or something to do with sports. But it has to be something they enjoy and look forward to. Something they can do all by themselves and feel good about.

The second goal should be a monthly goal. Something which takes a little more time, but not much, perhaps on an every other day basis. This goal should be one they are fairly interested in and will gain more knowledge from. You see, here we are stimulating them in wanting and having to know more about their subject. Perhaps it could be painting a picture, learning more information on a subject they have always wanted to know more about, or maybe it could be running an extra mile.

By achieving these goals which are relatively simple, they are learning OUTCOME and SATISFACTION with themselves. They are learning a little more self-esteem, and they are learning THEY CAN DO IT. THEY CAN MAKE IT. They are being stimulated, but the parent needs to participate along with them, therefore, adding support. No, these goals may not win awards . . . but they may at some point, someday, because they will have learned how to achieve and succeed in their efforts.

The third goal is a yearly goal. Again, it does not have to be a tough goal, for all our goals must be within reach of reality and achievement. It must be a goal we do not constantly have to work on, but one we will keep in the back of our minds. We will keep it in the back of our minds so when the time comes we can say, "Hey, I can put that towards my goal."

This yearly goal is a project, just as the smaller ones are; however, what this teaches us is follow-through . . . something many people do not know how to do. It gives us something to look forward to, and teaches us responsibility for ourselves . . . not others.

Our yearly goal could be putting together a collection, perhaps participating in a sport which will enrich us, or putting together a new dance routine . . . anything. For what this will do is give us a full year to think about one certain subject which relates to us. If we find we don't like this subject . . . fine . . . but we will have learned. We can pick a different topic for the next year, thus, bringing versatility into the forefront of our lives.

Personally, I absolutely LOVE versatility. And versatility comes into play during our young adult years. We can change jobs while we are young, because we have the ability to adapt. We can spend a year or two or three at one thing, learn all we can or want to know, and then find something else to become adept at. During each of these periods this versatility will have an affect on the outcome of the remainder of our lives . . . and we will have learned.

One aspect I fear is that we may actually be taking away or removing goals from our children. I can't tell you how many times I have heard people say,

"How am I ever going to find a job?"

"I want five more minutes for a lunch break."

"I want and I should have."

Who says you should? You, that's who. Times are rough and jobs are not easy to come by. But I'll give you two examples of close friends of mine. Both found themselves in positions where they HAD to find jobs. Both were females. Of course, they knew jobs were scarce, but were they put off? NO. They knew they had one thing to offer and one thing to sell . . . and that was . . . themselves.

Both thought, and finally came up with ideas of what they wanted to do and make a career of. They then both discovered there were absolutely no jobs available in each area. Did they back down? NO.

Each compiled lists of places offering what they wanted whether there were openings or not. Although there were no available spaces . . . they each MADE one for themselves. How did they do this? Well, they did not go into the office sobbing about how rough life was, or that someone owed them a chance or an opportunity in order to get them out of their situations. NO. They went in and said, "This is what I have to offer."

"I will give you hard work, and I will make a committment to you and your company."

"I will become an asset to you, and I will not bring you down."

Both had jobs created FOR them, and for more money than they ever thought possible. It says a little about attitude, doesn't it? Both were given jobs with more responsibility than they had ever had before.

People are willing to take chances, and are willing to take risks if they know you mean business and can produce. I would say 80 percent of the population expects someone to put out for THEM. They want more than what they are willing to give.

Sure, I may have wanted more money (greed is a human trait), but I was always glad I HAD a job. When anyone hires me I perceive it as THEIR taking a chance on ME. They are doing ME a favor. Therefore, they deserve the best I can do for THEM.

And now for a little philosophy on life. I said before, things or situations always came about or occurred for a reason . . . that being to drive or stimulate us into learning. Well, I also believe that a good life will COME to us if we LIVE a good life. Here again, we are dealing with attitudes . . . attitudes which want for nothing. I have learned from experience if I do something with the intention of NOT BENEFIT-

ING myself, things, people, or occurrences will benefit me threefold. It may not be monetarily (which it usually isn't), it may take a few years, but it will enrich my life and me somehow, someway.

I attempted to explain this theory to a friend at one time, but apparently he did not understand. A year later he approached me and said, "But when do I start getting back what I've given out?" Well, no wonder he was frustrated. For one thing, he was expecting a return. He was also giving away material items such as money and furniture. This is not what I meant.

You give of YOURSELF whether it be time, energy, or an idea in reference to helping another human being better THEMSELVES. It is not that you give someone else a free ride . . . nothing is for free. But you help open a few doors or avenues. You spend time putting yourself out (this IS giving) in many areas. What you receive back down the line is not a check in the mail, but someone opening a few avenues for you, avenues which will be very important to you at some point. It may even be in the form of a friendship when you need it the most. Good things will simply come to those who do good.

Take the classic example of driving down the freeway. It can be very nerve racking and very frustrating. Sometimes it feels like everyone is out to get you no matter what. Then you come to the old entrance ramp. Nobody is going to let you in. Then something miraculous happens, someone slows and actually waves you in. It makes your day! And what do you do? You let the next guy in. It takes shape in the form of practicing a way of life.

In our state we get a lot of snow. Oh boy . . . do we get a lot of snow. You can be out on any street in any part of town and ultimately . . . get stuck. We see this occurring at least 50 times per winter. Do you know what happens? People actually dive out of their cars with no jackets or boots on, and push you out or through. They could have gotten around you, but they chose to stop and help. Clocks are stopped, and time doesn't matter anymore. We're all in it together, and by George we'll make it through . . . somehow. We actually have FUN.

Once I went through a season of ten flat tires. I never once changed one myself, and do you know that during six of these flat tires I never even had time to get out of my car? Someone had already stopped to help.

I have even stopped in stores and found something I wanted to buy, but discovered I had left my purse at home. Do you know what they do? They give it to you anyway, and trust that you will send the money. These people are not naive or stupid . . . not by a long shot. (Studies indicate trusting people are more intelligent.) People are willing to take chances and risks if they know you believe in yourself. Self-esteem. This is what it is all about. We MUST teach it, and pass it on to our children.

THE WISH LIST

About a month ago Jessica bought her own pair of ice skates. She used birthday money and tooth fairy money to pay for them. She had thought about those ice skates for over a year, only I had always refused to buy them for her. It wasn't that I didn't want her to have ice skates, it was the timing of the asking. When the question of buying ice skates came up, it just happened to be the time when I would remind myself it was important to say "no" to things. She didn't hold it against me, she waited, and bought her own. Which reminds me of our wish list.

A wish list is something a parent can use to get a child to do what they want them to do. First of all, you have to wish for something; this is also a great goal-setting-reaching device. A child can even wish for three things, it doesn't matter. Then the parent thinks of what they are having problems with in regard to their child. The parent finally has their field day, they can think of anything. (But be reasonable.) It was really hard to decide, because you can only put down one thing at a time. I finally went with the old "picking up your room." Then you decide how many picking up the rooms there must be before they reach their goal. Jessica's goal at the time was a "Gem" doll. But your goals can be anything, it could even be extending curfews, items of clothing, etc.

You then make up a little chart and put checks or stars behind that one goal, such as:

CLEANING UP AFTER DINNER

Extra Curfew Hour	✔	✔	✔					
Esprit Pants	✔	✔						

Whatever chore you choose, it should be one that can be done daily so the child will be able to gauge his progress. We have used brushing teeth, practicing the piano, cleaning up the playroom, cleaning up your room, and getting dressed by yourself. What has happened with each one of these is that it became the norm. It became routine. Jessica began doing them because she was used to doing them. She was also meeting daily, weekly and monthly goals. And Mom was happier. I didn't have to think for half an hour on how I was going to manipulate her into doing something. It also instills consistency.

FEARS AND RESPONSIBILITY

Fear comes into focus within the realm of new responsibility. Children and young adults may not be setting or achieving their goals for the mere fact society has implanted the notion they are unobtainable. It offers us excuses.

If the young adult is 17 or 18 years old, he has many years of hard work ahead for him in looking towards his ultimate goal. Why should he even attempt to obtain this goal or even the smaller ones when the world will soon be blown up by nuclear weapons? This fear is very valid.

Not all adolescents are thinking of this dilemma, however, many are. There are portions or groups in society who participate and who practice survival in the case of nuclear war. What these groups do is make us wake up, stop and think.

"Why should I even go to school, let alone, finish school?"

"Why should I put out now if all my efforts will have been for nothing?"

"Maybe I should be out practicing survival for something I may really need."

"What's the point?"

You see, the trouble with current affairs or the news media is that it only portrays disaster, heartache, and destruction. But this is what it has to do, because this is what news is. Sure, we may see one success story or perhaps even two. However, the majority will be concentrated on persons out of work, persons on strike, murder, etc.

We may begin to perceive the adverse aspects as the NORM. Such as with so many people out of work. "I can't even be expected to find a job." "Why even try?" Or work a little, get laid off, and collect unemployment. "That's what everyone else is doing aren't they?" Everyone else is starving and complaining, so why shouldn't I?

Or the young adult attempts to find a job for two months and then we say, "Well, jobs are too hard to find. You tried and that is all that matters." However, here we are teaching them lack of perserverance.

Perserverance is a very hard aspect to learn, however, by our teaching them to achieve the smaller goals I believe perserverance will be brought forth. Goals just may take a little more time and a little more work, but they can be achieved no matter what they are.

As far as the world perhaps slipping into oblivion and self-destructing, this is an aspect we must deal with and address, because we do live in a nuclear age. We must get the point across that no matter what happens we HAVE to continue to travel through, attempting to reach our potential. It doesn't matter when or where death may come to us . . . today must be well lived in order for our existence to be acknowledged . . . if only to ourselves.

STRAIGHT FROM THE HORSE'S MOUTH

Five years ago I interviewed a group of students who were studying "Problems in American Society." Out of 50 students, approximately 20 chose to partake in answering the questions.

Recently, the Burns W. Roper company conducted a poll among 1,000 kids aged 8 through 17 for the American Chicle Group. In regard to fears of today's youngsters, kidnapping, threat of nuclear war, and fear of catching AIDS ranked very high. It also found out the following:

- 90 percent were happy with their home life.
- 93 percent were happy with their parents' love towards them.
- 79 percent thought the amount of time their parents spent with them was satisfactory.
- Out of the above category, 62 percent were happy with their relationships with their siblings.
- 39 percent felt they could talk openly with their parents.
- 18 percent wished their parents would spend less time on their personal lives.
- 14 percent wished their parents would spend more time on their personal lives.
- 3 percent wished their parents would spend less time with them.
- 62 percent said they would do no better or worse in school if their mothers worked. Seven percent said they would do better if they worked, and 26 percent said they would do worse..
- 40 percent said that kids get into more trouble if their mothers work.
- 47 percent said they are more independent if their mothers work.

QUESTION ONE

"What do you see as your biggest fear as you think about venturing out into the world on your own?"

(1) Eleven students responded with . . . not being able to find a job.

(2) Two replied, "Not having enough money to support myself."

(3) Not being able to afford a nice home.

(4) Not being able to handle everyday problems.

(5) Trying to get along with myself.

(6) Lack of money.

(7) Being able to afford food.

(8) Living by myself.

(9) Not relying on my parents anymore.

(10) How I am going to be able to afford to live.

(11) Going into the hospital and not being able to afford it.

(12) What I am going to do with my life.

(13) Having to resort to relying on my parents forever.

(14) What to do!

(15) Going away to college.

(16) Wondering if I will have enough money to support myself.

(17) Not making enough money to live how I want to live.

(18) SURVIVING! Being able to get a job and support myself.

QUESTION TWO

"What do you see as your largest responsibility as an individual?"

(1) To take care of myself and others.

(2) Not turning "sour."

(3) Making my parents happy.

(4) To support myself and my family.

(5) Being a good person and not hurting others.

(6) Being there for my loved ones who need me.

(7) Paying the rent and being happy.

(8) Being a good adult and getting along with others.

(9) To try my best in contributing towards helping others.

(10) To cut the "bull," money problems, and look at the people.

(11) Keeping a job.

(12) To succeed.

(13) To take care of whomever I am responsible for.

(14) To trust myself in whatever I chose to do.

(15) To do what is right for me and set a good example.

(16) Getting my schoolwork done.

(17) To be able to survive each day.

(18) To be able to survive and to keep the world alive.

(19) Being an individual . . . being ME! Doing things I want to do.

(20) To be fair and honest in my dealing with others. To support the things I believe in, but if I don't believe in something I should speak out.

(21) To take care of myself.

(22) Being an individual, getting good grades, and getting through to others clearly.

QUESTION THREE

"Do you find yourself worrying about being on your own?" Nine said, "Yes," and eleven replied, "No."

In additional comments the students responded with:

(1) Yes, but I have doubts about being able to afford it.

(2) Yes, but I think it may be lonely.

(3) Yes, because it is all going to be so new and different. I sometimes wonder if I'll be able to survive!

(4) No, I'm going to enjoy my freedom and privacy.

(5) No, I think it will be fun and *very* interesting.

(6) No, I feel pretty confident.

(7) No, I think I can handle it.

(8) No, because I am very independent and like to be on my own.

(9) No, because I know how to manage money and live independently.

QUESTION FOUR

"Have you thought about your goal setting? What you would like to accomplish as an individual?"

(1) Six replied, "Yes, to be successful in whatever I chose to do."

(2) Four replied, "Yes, I would like to get married, have a successful career, and to be happy."

(3) Yes, to make something of myself.

(4) Yes, but I keep changing my goals, and I'm still not sure of what I want to do.

(5) Yes, to be a good person, be happy, find the right spouse; and have a family.

(6) Six replied, "Yes, to go to college and be successful."

(7) Yes, to see places I have never been to, experience life and not let it pass me by. To be a good parent.

(8) Yes, to become an architect or an auto mechanic.

(9) No, I haven't thought about setting goals.

(10) No, I haven't thought much about that, but I want to go through school and get a good career I will like.

QUESTION FIVE

"If you have begun to anticipate these goals . . . do you fear there is a chance you cannot meet them because of the state of the world?"
Fourteen replied, "Yes," and five replied, "No."
In separate responses the comments were the following:

(1) Yes, the only thing is money.

(2) Yes, because I get scared of all the evil and hatred in the world. I need willpower. I get scared thinking about the lack of resources such as fuel and overcrowding, etc.

(3) Yes, because if I were to fail once I may not want to try again.

(4) Yes, when they talk about how the world is going downhill and of nuclear war.

(5) Yes, because not many people will be able to afford the things they need.

(6) Because the world is in such a mess now . . . who knows what it will be like in 15–20 years?

(7) Yes, for the state may be in total pandemonium, and my goals may never have a chance to become.

(8) No, it probably wouldn't be the world's fault if I don't achieve my goal.

(9) No, not really, because I don't see how the state of the world could stop me!

(10) No, for I have already begun to go for these goals. I am presently working two jobs and am going to school fulltime.

QUESTION SIX

"Do you fear there may be a nuclear war?"
Fourteen replied, "Yes," and five replied, "No."
Separate comments were the following:

(1) Yes, I am very afraid.

(2) Yes, it's inevitable.

(3) Yes, it would be so easy for someone to slip.

(4) Yes, I have heard many things, and I wonder if I am going to be able to fulfill my goals.

(5) Probably, but I am not going to worry about it, because there is not that much I can do when it comes.

(6) No, I don't think people would want to do that much damage to the world.

(7) No. Who cares? It happens . . . it happens.

(8) No, not in the near future.

(9) No, but if there is, it will happen, and there will not be much you can do about it . . . so why worry?

QUESTION SEVEN

"Do you plan to have a family and if not . . . why?"
Fourteen replied, "Yes," and three replied, "No."
The separate responses were the following:

(1) Yes, I want kids, and I want to take care of them.

(2) Yes, but I don't want a large family.

(3) Yes, when I can afford them.

(4) Yes, I want many children.

(5) Yes, because I love children.

(6) Yes, one child *if* my husband wants one.

(7) Yes, but not until I have lead a single life for a while.

(8) No, I want to be able to support myself first. When I am 26 I will decide.

(9) No, maybe marry, but I hate kids.

(10) No, because I don't want to have to worry about others.

QUESTION EIGHT

"Do you think your parents support you in your goal setting?"
Fifteen replied, "Yes," and four replied, "No."
Additional responses included the following:

(1) Yes, they give me courage and don't stand in my way.

(2) Yes, I am very lucky, because not only do my parents support me, but they help me make them come true.

(3) Yes, but I don't get much independence.

(4) Yes, but they tell me it will be difficult.

(5) Yes, they encourage me a lot, and it helps. They also have had money problems, and I think that is why I want to have a good job, because I know what they went through.

QUESTION NINE

"Do you view or regard yourself as an individual with unlimited potential?"

Eleven replied, "Yes," and seven replied, "No."

Separate comments are the following:

(1) Yes, I think I could do anything if I really tried.

(2) Yes, because whatever I set my mind to do, I will do it.

(3) Yes, if I can get past my hang-ups.

(4) Yes, I can do about anything if I put my mind to it.

(5) Yes, because if I find I can't do something, I can just do something else. I always have a choice.

(6) Yes, I have a lot of potential to a point, and I will put my best foot forward, help and try my hardest. But if I don't get any reward I will slack off.

(7) No, I don't think I could do everything.

(8) No, I can learn, but not at an unlimited potential.

QUESTION TEN

"Do you feel your parents or your support system fails you or perhaps dampens your dreams and desires?"

Thirteen replied, "Yes," and five replied, "No."

Additional comments were the following:

(1) Yes, I know it does!

(2) Yes, but I set my goals too high.

(3) Yes, but they usually do it without even knowing it.

(4) Yes, my parents fail me.

(5) Yes, because I am very independent for my age, and my parents think that I don't spend enough time at home.

(6) Yes, but I dream a lot and sometimes lose sense of reality.

(7) No, my friends support me.

(8) No, but when economics keep getting worse; reality always ruins my dreams.

SUMMARY

Adolescents . . . do not let it all overwhelm you, take it one step at a time. Take it one day at a time. Going through adolescence will probably be the most difficult time in your life. It will get easier, believe it or not. If you make it through adolescence with flying colors, you will probably be able to make it through anything. What you think is important today will not seem so a few years later. There will be other problems to solve, and you will solve them.

Out of all the people who surround you in your life right now, only two or three will remain as friends when you are older and out of school. Keep this in mind. They are only in your life for a short time. But these people, at this time, will try to influence you. You must be certain that each step you take, is the step you, and only you, wish to make. It does not even matter what your parents think, what matters is what YOU think. You are smart; you will use your brain, your heart, and the information you have accumulated up to this point. This information is enough for now, you have enough information to be able to choose wisely.

This may, at this time, be the most difficult time in history for an adolescent. The choices you make today will have a definite bearing on your future and the future of your children. This is not meant to scare you but to make you aware of the importance of your choices. These choices are not necessarily "decisions." Decisions are meant to be based on accumulated facts for a duration, or deliberation of time. Choices, in the terms I mean them, will have to be made instantly, they will be made daily—and you must have it set in your mind which direction, the final direction, you wish to go.

It won't make any difference to your friends what these choices will be. It won't make a great deal of difference to your parents . . . they will have their own choices to make. It WILL, however, make a difference to you and for you.

Even if we cannot see into the future, you must make your future a point of reference. You have to decide, today, if you want to have a life that is healthy. It all revolves around that one question.

Almost all of what we have talked about comes down to that one question. It depends on YOU and what YOU think of yourself. Do you think enough of yourself to be able to put all else aside . . . and do what you think you should do? THINK of all that is INSIDE of you: your individuality, your uniqueness. You are a very special being, and it is time you realized it. I say this sincerely. Do not let *anyone* put out that light shining within you, you must keep it burning even if it seems all is against you. All is not against you. It only matters if you think you are worth something—and you may multiply this worth at least tenfold in the end. You are "only" young at this time; we need your knowledge and your thoughts—what is in the heart of you . . . to sustain us for the future.

You must remember at all times: I am not an expert on your life. The experts are not the experts on your life. The only expert on your life is YOU.

> *While our today lurks*
> *In yesterday's shadow*
> *Our future will shine*
> *Only beyond tomorrow . . .*

INDEX